A Texas Suffragist

DIARIES AND WRITINGS OF JANE Y. McCALLUM

Edited by Janet G. Humphrey

Texas A&M University Press
College Station

LIBRARY OF CONGRESS CATALOGING-IN-PUBLICATION DATA

McCallum, Jane Y., author.
    A Texas suffragist: diaries and writings of Jane Y. McCallum / edited by Janet G.
Humphrey. — Texas A&M University Press edition.
        pages cm — (Women in Texas history series)
    First published by E.C. Temple in Austin, Texas, 1988.
    Includes bibliographical references and index.
    ISBN 978-1-62349-366-0 (pbk.: alk. paper) —
    ISBN 978-1-62349-367-7 (ebook)
    1. McCallum, Jane Y. 2. Suffragists—Texas—Biography.
3. Women—Suffrage—Texas—History. I. Humphrey, Janet G., 1943– editor.
II. Title. III. Series: Women in Texas history series.
    JK1899.M35A3 2015
    324.6'23092—dc23
    [B]
                                   2015023437

Publisher's Note: Please note that Jane Y. McCallum's writings appear intact, including
errors in spelling and punctuation.

Cover: The photograph of Jane Y. McCallum is courtesy of Betty Jane McCallum Ozbun.

A Texas Suffragist

Ellen C. Temple Classics in the
Women in Texas History Series

"We asked for the vote as a right denied. We never said that women would improve the world, though in our hearts we believed it."

JANE Y. MCCALLUM

NOTE ON THE AUTHOR

JANET G. HUMPHREY of Austin, Texas, received a B.A. degree from Swarthmore College and an M.A. degree in educational research from the University of Pittsburg. Her interest in history was inspired by reading documents as a research assistant rather than by her struggles to learn "the facts" as a student. She spent two years researching the Jane Y. McCallum Papers at the Austin History Center. This book is the happy result.

CONTENTS

ACKNOWLEDGMENTS

Although conducting research on Jane Y. McCallum has been genuinely enjoyable, the quest might not have been as fruitful without the help of a variety of people to whom I owe my thanks.

Members of the McCallum family were most gracious in granting permission to publish these materials and in providing details and answering questions: Fritz McCallum (Mrs. A. N., Jr.), Frances McCallum (Mrs. Henry), Betty Jane McCallum Ozbun, Jane Hardeman, and Janet Poage. Mrs. Ozbun, in addition, was especially generous in loaning me papers and photographs from her personal collection. The duties of courier fell to Mel Stockwell.

Current and former members of the staff of the Austin History Center often went out of their way to be helpful, particularly as we stumbled through the McCallum Papers, Part II: Linda Zezulka, Karen Warren, May Schmidt, Mary Jo Cooper, Jan Root, Bill Brock, and Bruce Jensen. I welcomed the encouragement from curator Audray Bateman Randle and am grateful for her reading of my manuscript.

I am indebted to Professor Lewis L. Gould for his time and thoughtful comments and acknowledge the support of Kate Adams and Judith N. McArthur with thanks. Without the commitment of Ellen C. Temple to broadcast the story of the woman suffrage movement in Texas, this publication might still be in a drawer. She has both my gratitude and admiration.

My children, Justin and Douglas, have endured the same benign neglect as did Jane McCallum's, and I appreciate their indulgence during the past two years. My husband David should know that his standards of research and writing have been my models from the outset of this project. His gentle guidance and understanding are reflected on each page.

JANET G. HUMPHREY

FOREWORD

Many accomplishments comprise the long life of Jane Y. McCallum: journalist, author, civic leader, suffragist, organizer, lobbyist, Texas Secretary of State, wife, and mother. Fortunately for readers, she also wrote prolifically, leaving behind a record of her observations as well as her deeds. McCallum is best known for her efforts, along with those of Minnie Fisher Cunningham and other members of the Texas Equal Suffrage Association (TESA), to win—at last—the vote for Texas women. The task in Texas took 52 years, having begun in 1868 with a failed request of the Constitutional Convention by a small group of women to confer the franchise upon them. By 1918, when TESA and its supporters finally succeeded, many other pro-suffrage groups had come and gone, as had several more unsuccessful attempts to persuade the Texas Legislature to pass a suffrage bill.

What finally made the difference? The well-organized, grass-roots campaign that Cunningham and McCallum waged, galvanizing women across the state and building on growing support from groups like the Women's Christian Temperance Union, the Texas Federation of Women's Clubs, the Texas Federation of Colored Women's Clubs, and from prominent men like S. P. Brooks, the president of Baylor University, and Charles Metcalfe, a member of the Texas House of Representatives.

McCallum's tenacity, intelligence, and wit are all on display in Janet G. Humphrey's carefully annotated collection of McCallum's diaries and writings, a project that took Humphrey two years to complete. First published in 1988 by Ellen C. Temple, *A Texas Suffragist* is a fine companion to *Citizens at Last: The Woman Suffrage Movement in Texas* (edited by Temple, Judith McArthur, and Ruthe Winegarten), another Temple publication that had been published in 1987. Together, these volumes provide the personal perspective and the overview necessary to more fully understand one of the most significant social and political changes to occur in Texas history—the official recognition of women's right to their own voice as citizens. That these two books were published at virtually the same time is thanks in part to the fact that the four women who produced them knew each other and understood the significance of their research to the emerging field of Texas women's history. The original publication of these two books is also due to Ellen Temple's dedication to educating the public about the historic achievement that winning the vote represented.

The editors of Texas A&M University Press's Women in Texas History Series are proud to make *A Texas Suffragist: Diaries and Writings of Jane Y. McCallum*, by Janet G. Humphrey, available once again as part of its Ellen C. Temple Classics of Texas Women's History collection.

Nancy Baker Jones and Cynthia J. Beeman
Series Editors

INTRODUCTION

Since her death in 1957, Jane Y. McCallum's life of nearly eighty years has taken on luster. Although recognized during her lifetime as a civic leader and courted by politicians from William P. Hobby to Lyndon Johnson, the extent of her contributions is only recently becoming acknowledged. A resident of Austin for most of her adulthood, McCallum was continually involved in the political life of the Texas capital—as suffragist, campaigner, lobbyist, and eventually Texas Secretary of State. As a journalist and author she voiced her opinions on issues of current interest and reminded her readers of the countless ways that women have enriched society.

That Jane Y. McCallum wrote for publication, corresponded, took notes, and kept diaries makes possible this self-portrait of her life through 1919. The heart of this volume is her two diaries for the period from October 1916 through December 1919, reprinted in Parts II and III. They provide a full and unaffected portrayal of McCallum during the climactic years of the woman suffrage movement in Texas and place it in the context of World War I and the era of progressive reform. Excerpts from her newspaper columns and her suffrage campaign publicity work complete the story of these years. The documents brought together in Part I form the prelude to her suffrage activities. McCallum's descriptions of her grandmothers, her early married life, and her children's first years help to set the stage for what would become a career of public service lasting four decades.

PUBLIC CAREER

Jane LeGette Yelvington's life began on her parents' ranch in LaVernia (Wilson County), Texas, in 1878. Her marriage to Arthur Newell McCallum a mere eighteen years later marked the start of her responsibilities as an adult. A teacher's wife, and upon her husband's promotion, the wife

3

of the school superintendent in Kenedy, Texas, she soon became the mother of a daughter.

The earliest signs of Jane McCallum's abundant energy and "urge to do what she could in return for the gift of life"[1] were her women's club memberships and civic work in Kenedy and Seguin, Texas, where the McCallums relocated in 1901.

When the family, which by then counted four children, moved to Austin in 1903, Jane Y. McCallum was the wife of the school superintendent in a city of over 22,000 people.[2] She joined several women's clubs and enrolled in courses at the University of Texas. By the time her fifth and youngest child was well established in school, she had enlisted in the Austin Woman Suffrage Association. This local chapter of about seventy-five members was affiliated with state and national organizations devoted to winning the vote for women.

Between 1915 and 1919 McCallum's daily life was dominated by her involvement in events of statewide and national significance. To her, as to many women, World War I meant immersing herself in the work on the home front: selling Liberty Bonds, aiding a recruitment drive, protecting soldiers at Texas camps from immoral conditions, and conserving food and other commodities more urgently needed in Europe.

The uproar created by Governor James E. Ferguson's attempt to take control of the University of Texas in 1917 provided McCallum with her first opportunity to leave a mark on gubernatorial politics. McCallum already counted herself staunchly in the anti-Ferguson camp because of his opposition to woman suffrage and prohibition and was eager to join with other proponents of reform. She took a vocal stance on the side of the University and a leading role in the successful 1918 election campaign of Ferguson's opponent, William P. Hobby.

Above all during these years, the woman suffrage movement reached its culmination, and Jane McCallum figured conspicuously among a handful of state leaders. Her speeches and legislative lobbying in 1918 were instrumental in winning primary suffrage for Texas women. She led a massive publicity campaign for full suffrage in 1919 and lobbied successfully for Texas's prompt ratification of the federal woman suffrage amendment.

[1]Untitled biographical note, p. 3, folder on research notes and articles, McCallum Papers, Part II, Austin History Center, Austin Public Library (hereafter cited as McCP, II). (As of January 1987, the processing of the McCallum Papers, Part II was incomplete. Therefore it is not possible to give a reliable citation for the location of many documents in this collection.)

[2]Census data for 1900 published in *Texas Almanac and State Industrial Guide: 1974-1975* (Dallas, 1973), 186.

The issue of woman suffrage presented McCallum with her first chance to test the waters of journalism. She contributed a weekly column to the local newspaper between 1917 and 1919 which reported state and national suffrage news, countered arguments from opponents, and related anecdotes. She later wrote a book, published in 1929, entitled *Women Pioneers* which she believed filled a gap in American history texts by pointing up the contributions of colonial American women.

For several years after the strenuous suffrage campaigns, McCallum could not be lured away from her family. But in 1923 she accepted the position as executive secretary of the Women's Joint Legislative Council (JLC). Initially composed of representatives of five well-respected state women's organizations, the group was dedicated to promoting legislation that reflected the concerns of women. One can imagine Jane McCallum's delight in the council's nickname, the Petticoat Lobby.

The JLC flourished under McCallum's hand. During the sessions of 1923 and 1925, the legislature enacted much of its agenda, in part due to the lobbying and publicity she supervised. The JLC supported stronger prohibition and child labor laws, improvements in the penal and educational systems, and a program for maternal and infant health care.[3]

McCallum's interest in prison reform led to her appointment to the Texas Committee on Prisons and Prison Labor. Among a number of improvements which the committee recommended to the legislature in the 1920s were centralized, more responsible management and more humane conditions.[4]

By 1926 many Texas women were united in their determination to defeat Governor Miriam A. Ferguson in her reelection bid. For two years they had watched her attend mainly to her household duties while her husband, their old nemesis, ran the executive branch. When the state attorney general, Dan Moody, announced he would oppose the "two governors for the price of one," the women were in business. Prodded by many of her friends to accept, Jane McCallum became head of the Texas Women Citizens' Committee, Dan Moody for Governor.

In recognition of the role the women had played in his election, Moody named Jane Y. McCallum his secretary of state. She agreed somewhat

---

[3]Walter Prescott Webb, H. Bailey Carroll, and Eldon Stephen Branda, eds., *The Handbook of Texas*, 3 vols. (Austin, 1952, 1976), 2:929; Jane Y. McCallum (hereafter cited as JYM), "Women In Politics," *London Times*, Texas Supplement, Mar. 30, 1925, p. ix. See also Emma Louise Moyer Jackson, "Petticoat Politics: Political Activism Among Texas Women in the 1920's" (Ph.D. diss., University of Texas at Austin, 1980).

[4]Norman D. Brown, *Hood, Bonnet, and Little Brown Jug: Texas Politics, 1921-1928* (College Station, 1984), 261-62.

reluctantly, fearful, she wrote, "lest some individual might think I *wanted a job*"[5] and that this ambition, rather than her desire for clean government, had motivated her work in Moody's campaign.

During her six years in office, McCallum modernized archaic procedures and equipment in the secretary of state's department. But the most familiar story from these years is of her discovery of one of the original copies of the Texas Declaration of Independence. She consulted with experts for advice on preserving the document and, together with a legislative committee, created a shrine in the Capitol for its display.[6]

Governor Ross Sterling, who had appointed McCallum to a third term as secretary of state, failed in his try for reelection in the 1932 primary. As Jane McCallum witnessed the return of the Fergusons to the governor's mansion in January 1933, she could not contain her feelings: "Some how, there was a suggestion of slinking things that creep out from under stones and chips and dead leaves."[7]

Later in the 1930s, after a period of ill health, McCallum resumed the normal pace of her activities. She was elected state historian of the Society of Colonial Dames in Texas and a board member of the Travis County Council of Women, a group whose programs in home economics and public health were aimed at improving the welfare of county residents. Her efforts in planning and raising funds assured the Austin-Travis County community of a tuberculosis sanitorium.

Continually occupied with local Democratic party politics, McCallum was a presidential elector in 1940. She campaigned in Congressman Lyndon Johnson's U.S. Senate races in 1941 and 1948, and in 1942 served as Moody's state chairman for the Dan's the Man for Senate committee in addition to her membership on the state Democratic executive committee. She actively supported her suffrage colleague Minnie Fisher Cunningham in an unsuccessful bid for the governor's mansion in 1944. The next year she began a seven-year stint on the Austin Planning Commission.

In some respects the decade of the 1940s must have seemed like *déjà vu* to Jane McCallum. That her life would twice be affected by a world war and a simultaneous major crisis at the University of Texas was a singular

[5]JYM diary, Jan. 10, 1927, in the possession of Betty Jane McCallum Ozbun, Austin, Texas.

[6]Typescript from *Dallas Morning News*, Mar. 2, 1930, feature section, Jane Y. McCallum Papers, Barker Texas History Center, University of Texas at Austin; *Biennial Report of the Secretary of State of the State of Texas: September 1, 1929 to September 1, 1930* (Austin, n.d.), 9-20.

[7]JYM diary, Jan. 17, 1933, Series A.2, McCP, I.

coincidence. McCallum's feelings toward the villains of World War II were as vehement as her earlier views of Kaiser Wilhelm: "like animals with rabies [—] all snarling, snapping starving & torturing maiming murdering their fellow beings that they may obtain power and more power."[8] Her uneasiness increased when her son Brown enlisted in the naval reserves in 1942 and was on active duty within months.[9]

The Rainey controversy at the University of Texas boiled over when the Board of Regents fired President Homer Price Rainey in November 1944 because of basic philosophical differences and his refusal to dismiss several faculty members.[10] As in the Ferguson battle of 1917, the academic community arose in defense of its highly respected leader. Texas women, with Jane Y. McCallum in the forefront, organized the Women's Committee for Educational Freedom in January 1945. Using the by now familiar tactics of statewide petition and letter writing drives, intensive lobbying of legislators, and well-publicized speeches and meetings, the group sought to win Rainey's reinstatement and the resignations of regents who voted for his dismissal.[11] The Board of Regents prevailed in the end, despite the committee's strong and constructive voice.

Even in her later years McCallum adhered to her philosophy of middle age: "Partake of its poise, judgment, wisdom, but, — while it will place a *dimmer* on your youthful ecstacies, never submit to an *extinguisher*."[12] She enjoyed social activities, several clubs, her garden, and most especially the visits from her children and grandchildren. In 1954, when Jane Y. McCallum was seventy-five, the Texas constitution was amended to allow women to serve on juries. Travis County appointed her its first female grand jury commissioner four days after the amendment went into effect.[13] At her death in August 1957 a newspaper tribute pointed out that her career drew attention to "the remarkable change in the public attitude toward women as citizens which has taken place within the span of one lifetime."[14]

[8]JYM Record Book, Jan. 28, 1939, in the possession of Betty Jane McCallum Ozbun.
[9]Typed note on personalized JYM stationery, n.d., folder on World War II, McCP, II.
[10]Joe B. Frantz, *The Forty-Acre Follies* (Austin, 1983), 81-85; Ronnie Dugger, *Our Invaded Universities: Form, Reform, and New Starts* (New York, 1974), 36-47.
[11]"Women's Committee on Educational Freedom, Minutes of Meeting Held in Austin January 18, 1945," Series A.5, McCallum Papers, Part I, Austin History Center, Austin Public Library (hereafter cited as McCP, I); *Austin Statesman*, Jan. 18, 1945, p. 1; *Austin American-Statesman*, Jan. 27, 1945, pp. 1, 7.
[12]JYM, "How I Think Middle age Should be Met," p. 5, short stories folder, McCP, II.
[13]*Austin American-Statesman*, Nov. 24, 1954, p. 1.
[14]*Austin American-Statesman*, Aug. 16, 1957, p. 4.

PERSONAL PORTRAIT

Despite the expanded opportunities for women during the first half of the twentieth century, which Jane McCallum had both fostered and turned to good account, she claimed in 1950 that her outstanding achievement was "My family."[15] She found being a wife, a mother, and a homemaker no less fulfilling than her other endeavors. Whether chaperoning a dance, cheering for her son's football team, hiking, or overseeing homework, she simply delighted in motherhood. The drudgery entailed in raising a daughter and four sons, born over a nine year span, was inconsequential compared to the rewards they gave her. She watched them mature with pride, tolerance, and a certain anxiety, both encouraging them to strive and allowing them the freedom to stumble.

McCallum sought throughout her adulthood to strike a balance between her public career and her family life. During her twenties and early thirties her social and civic activities were less central to her routine, but still attracted her interest. When she was about forty, her efforts in behalf of woman suffrage overshadowed her roles as mother and homemaker. Then in 1921 she refused the chairmanship of the Joint Legislative Council, saying she was "needed at home."[16] Yet she was determined not to be "a *barnacle* in the world."[17] She warned her children not to offer her "a comfy space on this shelf" where they could expect her to "sit and do tatting or play bridge" for her remaining years.[18]

One occupation which McCallum found compatible with domesticity was writing. She wrote and wrote, and, equally important, she saved much of what she wrote. From reading her papers and the comments of her contemporaries, an impression of her personality emerges. Jane Y. McCallum was a forceful, lively person. She was brim full of a zest for whatever life offered. In her bold, upright handwriting, sprinkled with dashes and underscorings, she extolled the wildflowers and lambasted the Kaiser.

She could express her strong, yet thoughtful, opinions orally as well. In 1924, when Governor Pat Neff declined McCallum's request to designate a peace week in Texas, she threatened to give him a piece of her mind. She quotes him as replying, "Well, if I remember correctly, it will

[15]*Austin American*, Jan. 8, 1950, sect. B, p. 7.
[16]JYM diary, Jan. 24, 1921, Series A.2, McCP, I.
[17]Untitled biographical note, p. 6, folder on research notes and articles, McCP, II.
[18]JYM, "How I Think Middle age Should be Met," p. 8, miscellaneous folder, McCP, II. (The pages of this essay were in two folders.)

not be the *first* time. You have stood me in a corner a number of times &
told me what you thought of me. Why not tell me now again?"[19]

After observing elected public officials over many years, McCallum
concluded that "some *grew; too many swelled!*"[20] She was usually among
the first to point out the humorous side of a situation. But it was people
she found most amusing. In an undated handwritten comment beside a
photograph of a candidate for governor, McCallum noted, "men are so
funny when [they] try to look stern and important!"[21] McCallum enjoyed
clever wit, whether it was her own or someone else's. Anecdotes, quips,
and humorous observations are scattered throughout her writings.

Some of what she witnessed, on the other hand, was in no way
humorous. Possessed of a strong sense of justice, McCallum was an
ardent defender of those whom she felt had been treated unfairly. She
stood by people she knew, such as University of Texas faculty members
faced with dismissal, or her close friend Nell Doom, whose house had
been undervalued at a condemnation hearing.[22] To McCallum, denying
women the vote, excluding them from juries, misleading Texas farmers
with empty promises, and allowing impoverished mothers and their
infants to receive inadequate medical care were all injustices that demanded correction.

McCallum was as stern a critic of herself as she was of others. Marginal
notes made years later indicate that she was appalled at some of her
earlier writing. She questioned whether she had given her children
appropriate guidance. In 1919 she expressed doubts about her compe-
tence in leading a statewide political organization.[23]

One wonders whether McCallum was unsure of her abilities, particularly in the public arena, or whether she simply did not want to be
suspected of any sort of conceit. There are numerous examples of her
hesitancy in accepting responsibilities that would put her in the lime-
light. It is as though she relied on others' confidence in her, rather than
her certainty that she was the best person for the task.[24]

[19]JYM diary, Mar. 25, 1924, Series A.2, McCP, I.
[20]JYM to Henry and Frances McCallum ("Dear Ones"), Apr. 2, 1952, McCP, II.
[21]"Speech of Honorable Robert E. Lee Knight. . . ," Series G, #114, McCP, I.
[22]JYM diary, Aug. 11, 1924, Series A.2, McCP, I.
[23]JYM to Ella Dibrell ("Dear Lady"), Aug. 10, 1919, folder of letters from various people
on suffrage to and from JYM, 1916-1925, McCP, II.
[24]In her diary McCallum recorded her apprehension at the prospect of leading Dan
Moody's gubernatorial campaign and virtually surrendered to her friend Nell Doom's
forceful insistence. "Mrs. S. J. Smith, Nell, Miss Gearing and others are using every
argument to me to let them push me for Chairman for the women. It turns my heart to lead
to think about it. I'd much rather do the publicity and head [a] committee on literature.
. . . How *can* I do this thing. But Nell *has come to* life and woe is me, unless I can get her on

Members of McCallum's family were the first to reassure her in these situations. It was evident to all who knew him that Arthur McCallum, Sr., gave his complete support to his wife's activities—from joining the local suffrage group to accepting the appointment as Texas secretary of state. Throughout their life together he encouraged her to assume extra-familial responsibilities that gave her pleasure: a rare and precious quality in a husband in the early decades of the century. Her children, too, were proud of her adventures and accomplishments. A colleague later wrote to McCallum that she never forgot McCallum's "beautiful laughing, teasing face in the ante-chamber to the House with the 'army' [husband plus four sons] in the background to give you the security you needed."[25]

Not merely a narrator of significant events of the late nineteen-teens, Jane McCallum is an appealing figure in her own right. In an era when hemlines had just recently been raised above the ankles, most respectable ladies did not publicly embroil themselves in political controversies. Nor did they "race down Capital Hill to [the] Court House" and interrupt proceedings to speak with the judge.[26] As a prominent civic-minded woman in her thirties, the wife of the superintendent of Austin Public Schools, the mother of draft-age sons during a world war, Jane McCallum was uniquely involved in the years she called "these troublous times."[27]

DIARIES AND WRITINGS

McCallum's written legacy is vast. In addition to her innumerable newspaper columns and articles, contributions to edited works, and book on pioneer women, there are two collections of her papers at the Austin History Center and one in private hands.[28] These unpublished

the trail of some one else" (JYM diary, Mar. 13 [1926], Series A.2, McCP, I). The following year she commented on pressure from a "delegation of women" urging her to accept the appointment as secretary of state. "Mamma willing and *Hubby* also. What *shall* I do?" (JYM diary, Jan. 9, 1927, in the possession of Betty Jane McCallum Ozbun).

    25Editor's interview with Fritz McCallum, Frances McCallum, and Janet Poage, Mar. 5, 1986; Minnie Fisher Cunningham to JYM, Feb. 7, 1956, Series E, McCP, I.

    26JYM, "Nell & Others," 3-4, McCP, II. The story McCallum relates is that when she and a friend discovered that the primary suffrage resolution had not been put on the Senate calendar as Judge Paul Page, state senator from Bastrop, had promised, they called him out of his courtroom. He discovered the paper still in his pocket, and the women gave it to the calendar clerk.

    27JYM diary, June 15, 1917, Series A.2, McCP, I.

    28See the section titled "Published Works of Jane Y. McCallum" for a list of these items. The extent of diary material is indicated in the chronology. The bibliography contains additional details of several collections of McCallum's papers.

papers include a huge assortment of materials ranging from the trivial to the substantial: social invitations, autobiographical sketches, compositions she wrote for university courses, genealogical information, family correspondance, newspaper clippings, minutes of meetings, political campaign materials, copies of speeches she made, rough drafts of articles, research notes, formal committee reports, correspondance and financial records of the Texas Equal Suffrage Association, and personal diaries. They span the period from the 1890s to the 1950s and cover nearly every organization and cause that captured McCallum's interest.

Most illuminating in conveying her story, however, are the diaries. Those that have survived vary in richness, but represent a fair sampling of her adult years. One gets the sense that keeping a diary was both an outlet for her feelings and a means of recording events she wished to remember. The writing style is free and informal. She made note of her experiences, her impressions, and her emotions as time afforded. A number of entries end abruptly because she was interrupted by something more pressing. The long intervals between entries are disappointing, since they leave the reader in the dark about her reactions to some events. McCallum never mentioned Governor James Ferguson's eventual impeachment or the satisfaction it must have given her. Her account of a vacation trip in 1921 consists entirely of her diary entry for August 13: "Arrived here yesterday." The next note is dated March 1922.[29] Nevertheless, the diaries contain a priceless portrait.

EDITORIAL PROCEDURES

Unless otherwise noted, Jane Y. McCallum is the author of the documents reproduced here. She either wrote the material before 1920, or it concerns this period of her life. The two major sources for this self-portrait are McCallum's diaries for October 13, 1916, through July 20, 1918 (McCallum Papers, Part I, Austin History Center), and for 1919 (in the possession of Betty Jane McCallum Ozbun, Austin). This transcription follows the order of the pages in the original diaries with one or two exceptions which are noted in the text.

The diaries are reprinted in their entirety, except for two fragmentary false starts (at the end of the entry for October 30, 1916, and the beginning of the June 14, 1919 entry) and a number of legible words which McCallum crossed out in manuscript documents. I have retained mate-

---

[29]JYM diary, Aug. 13, 1921, and Mar. 13, 1922, Series A.2, McCP, I.

rial originally crossed out when it added to the content or style of the piece.

Other manuscripts not identified as excerpts appear in complete form. Footnotes give the rationale for deleting material by ellipses.

By liberal use of footnotes I have clarified Jane McCallum's references to people, places, and events and provided additional elaboration when it seemed useful. I have also introduced background narrative to provide a context for the larger issues that concerned McCallum. In addition, all the material contained within square brackets is my responsibility. I have kept the original spelling, capitalization, and punctuation, including errors, in both manuscript and previously published works. My objective has been to preserve McCallum's original words and style and, at the same time, to make the reading easier and less ambiguous.

Material which McCallum underscored in her writing appears here in italics. If only some of the letters in a word were underscored, the entire word is italicized here. Judgments are extremely fine and often impossible to make in most cases, and one can argue that the author usually intended to underline the entire word. I have retained a few exceptions where McCallum's emphasis on part of a word was clearly purposeful, such as her reference to suffragist "Mrs. Tru*man* Kelly." McCallum's distinction between underscoring several consecutive words with one line and with separate lines for each word is lost in the translation to print.

Although McCallum used dashes of greatly varying lengths, they are standardized here. To duplicate the original paragraphing requires making many individual judgments, since McCallum's indentations are often minute, particularly on the small diary pages. My intent has been to be faithful to the manuscript, but it is a subjective undertaking.

PART 1

REACHING MATURITY

The story of Jane Yelvington McCallum's formative years does not begin with her emergence as a suffragist or her marriage or even her birth. Rather, it begins with the ancestors of whom she was so proud. Her maternal forebears, the DeRossets, who settled in North Carolina about 1735, were distinguished enough to gain her membership in the Colonial Dames in Texas.[1] McCallum wanted her children, and later her grandchildren, to know of their heritage and to share her respect for their family.[2]

McCallum's paternal grandparents, Henry and Sarah Catherine Yelvington, migrated to Texas from Mississippi in 1851, when her father was a year old.[3] In addition to their household goods, they brought with them three slaves, farming equipment, seeds, and the cuttings of shrubs. They intended to farm acreage near Lockhart, but malaria drove them from the area three years later. The Yelvingtons resettled along the Cibolo Creek near LaVernia in Wilson County, about forty miles east of San Antonio.[4]

Jane McCallum recalled her Yelvington grandmother in an account written in the early 1950s, which she included as the final chapter in her unpublished manuscript on the courage of Texas women pioneers, *All Texians Were Not Males*. She remembered "a dyed-in-the-wool, dipped-under-the water Baptist": "a neat, comely, old lady—extending capable, still shapely though toil-worn, hands to some one in need, and saying quietly but firmly, 'Let me help you.'" McCallum continued, "She comforted the sorrowful, prayed with and for those 'still unsaved,' fed the preachers, nursed the sick, 'spoke her mind' on

---

[1] Colonial Dames material, McCP, II.

[2] JYM's will, folder on JYM's marriage and death, McCP, II.

[3] Typed notes on JYM stationery, Colonial Dames material, McCP, II; obituary of Alvaro Yelvington, newspaper clipping, n.d., folder on Alvaro and Mary Yelvington, McCP, II.

[4] JYM, "My Grandmothers," 495-96, short stories folder, McCP, II. There are two slightly different versions of this essay.

controversial issues when others held back, and could deliver a baby 'as good as any doctor,' when occasion demanded."[5]

McCallum admired her Grandma's pluck in this favorite anecdote. The incident occurred while her grandfather was away during the Civil War, and Sarah Yelvington remained home to run the farm.

Two burly men, dressed in worn Yankee uniforms and evidently deserters bent on looting if not worse, came blustering up on the front porch one day. Feigning fear, Grandma shrank back to where she could reach something that leaned against the wall just inside the door. Quick as a flash the intruders were looking down the double barrels of a shot gun, and being ordered to "About face—March" in tones that brooked no refusal. They marched.

After shuffling a mile up the sandy road, the ruffians found themselves at the McAllister home facing two armed men[,] Messrs B & C[,] who had [?] taken in the situation from afar and who promptly took them in charge.

As their captor turned to hurry back to her children, "Mr. Billy" (McAllister) called out, "Better be a little more careful how you handle that gun, hadn't you, Mrs. Yelvington?"

Our grandmother's nonchalant reply as she looked back over her shoulder was sorter startling, to say the least: "Oh, it's not loaded!"[6]

Like the Yelvingtons, Jane McCallum's maternal relatives were southerners who arrived in Texas in the 1850s. The LeGettes, however, were more aristocratic and accustomed to living in the "grand style." Catherine Maria LeGette or Grandmère, as she was called in deference to her French lineage, was an Episcopalian. McCallum believed her charitable manner originated in a sense of *noblesse oblige*. She came to Texas from South Carolina in December 1856 as a widow with eight children. The family took up residence in Seguin, where Catherine's brother had built a home.[7]

Jane McCallum described her Grandmère as "merry, witty and quick at repartee," even when she was in her seventies. She "apparently looked upon dancing as an essential part of a well-rounded, happy life," advising a grandchild, "Never take more on your heart, my dear, than you can dance off at your heels."[8]

[5] Ibid., 496, 497.
[6] Ibid., 497-98.
[7] Ibid., 500, 501.
[8] Ibid., 498-99.

In looking back, even McCallum was surprised that the children of "such contrasting families" had married. Mary Fullerton LeGette and Alvaro Leonard Yelvington, Jane McCallum's parents, spent most of their lives in LaVernia. Alvaro was born in 1850; Mary about 1854. The couple married in 1874 and maintained a farm-ranch. McCallum's father was at one time the sheriff of Wilson County when, according to his obituary, " 'bad men' were thick as flies."[9]

Of the six Yelvington children, Jane, born December 30, 1878, was the eldest to survive. She later remarked, "From all accounts I was a 'spoiled brat,' mainly (spoiled) because my little brother died 3 months before my birth."[10] The three daughters and two sons eventually married and went their separate ways, but they remained close. Since each continued to live in Texas, they corresponded and visited with some regularity.

The cupboard of available documents from Jane McCallum's child-hood is virtually bare. She was born in LaVernia and attended Wilson County schools and a Mississippi finishing school, Zealey's Female College.[11]

One letter that McCallum wrote when she was sixteen has survived. It was returned to the sender for old times' sake in 1948 by the recipient, a Mrs. McDaniel. Already in evidence is McCallum's habit of under-scoring words for emphasis.

LaVernia
Oct 10 - 1894

My dear Mamie:

It is Sunday evening. I have'nt been out of the house all day and am *lonesome* and want to see you so I am going to write. Mamie[,] after you left Thursday 27th I realized for the first time what realy was taking place. Before that I was so concerned about *your* happiness that I nearly forgot myself and how I would miss you. But when I did realize that you were *married* and *gone* words cant describe how *lost* I felt and feel yet[,] but then I know how happy *you* are and try not to think about it. Tell that husband of yours I could tie a stone to his neck and sink him in the Atlantic and

[9] Ibid., 495; obituary of Alvaro Yelvington, newspaper clipping, n.d., folder on Alvaro and Mary Yelvington, McCP, II; obituary of Mary Yelvington, clipping from the *Floresville Chronicle-Journal*, Dec. 28, 1934, folder on Alvaro and Mary Yelvington, McCP, II.

[10] JYM's "exact excerpt" of letter from Alvaro Leonard Yelvington to his sister Victoria Yelvington Lawhon, Jan. 15, 1903, with comments, folder on Alvaro and Mary Yelvington, McCP, II.

[11] *Handbook of Texas*, 3:552.

that I will carry my threat into execution if he dont bring you over real soon cause I have *so* much I want to talk to you about.

"Dontcherknow" there is a possibility of my getting to go to Laredo this Xmas! I am just *wild* to go and Mamma says I may provided she can "fix me up" to suit her. Wouldn't that be splendid tho? But please dont mention it to anyone[. I] dont suppose you would, but you *might* to Mattie or Josie and I have particular reasons for not telling anyone.

The LaVernia news (or my part) consists of a call from *Ed*[,] a trip to the Springs and Zeke was up last night. I declare I am realy afraid I will injure my health by dissipateing so much. Think I shall have to go to some "secluded spot" and rest up a while. (Laredo for instance)

Now *do* write to me real soon and tell me "just lots" I know you *could* write fifteen pages if you *would* and think you might think about how lonely it is for me and write them. As it is so dark I cant possibly see the lines I will close.

Love and best wishes to you both.

Your loving friend
Janie Y.[12]

Jane McCallum's comment penciled on the letter reflects on this period of her life from her perspective at age seventy.

Guess life was *rather dull* with few congenial spirits, though I only recall a singing eager, hopeful heart—parents strict as to associates and staid conventions.

If this lonely adolescent had known that about two years after sending this letter she, too, would be married, her mood might have lightened. Enter Arthur Newell McCallum.

McCallum was traveling west to California from his North Carolina home when he made a fateful stop in Texas. He became acquainted with a cousin of Jane Yelvington's and his trip ended in LaVernia.[13]

Born in 1865 of well-to-do parents, Arthur McCallum received a B.A. from Davidson College in North Carolina in 1887. He taught high

[12] JYM to Mamie McDaniel, Oct. 10, 1894, personal and business folder, McCP, II.

[13] Dorothy Boone, "Arthur Newell McCallum," typescript, 3, AF-Biography, Arthur Newell McCallum, Austin History Center, Austin Public Library (referred to hereafter as AHC, APL); Patricia B. Nieuwenhuizen, "Minnie Fisher Cunningham and Jane Y. McCallum, Leaders of Texas Women for Suffrage and Beyond" (Senior thesis, University of Texas at Austin, 1982), 20, Barker Texas History Center, University of Texas at Austin.

school Greek and Latin for one year, then helped on his family's plantation until he left for the west in 1895. Once in LaVernia, a town of 343 people in 1900, he accepted the position as principal of the high school.[14]

He and Jane Yelvington were married on October 29, 1896, when he was thirty-one and she was two months shy of eighteen. A newspaper announcement of their wedding glorified the match, reporting that the bride "represents all that the most fastidious could demand. [She is b]eautiful of face and figure, replete with that graciousness that makes Southern women so fascinating, and blessed with that kind disposition and noble character which make womanhood glorious. Prof. McCallum . . . fell heir to the noble, generous, chivalric disposition of his fore-parents, and holds the enviable reputation of being the embodiment of all that makes manhood honorable."[15]

Responsibilities grew for the couple within the first year of their marriage. Arthur McCallum was named superintendent of schools in Kenedy, Texas, where they moved in 1897, and the couple became the parents of their first child and only daughter, Kathleen. The family added a son, Alvaro Yelvington, in 1900 and moved to the town of Seguin, where Arthur became superintendent of a larger school district. Their third child, Arthur Newell, Jr., was born in 1901.[16]

Later, perhaps during the 1930s, Jane McCallum's diversion when ill with a cold was to write of the family's years in Kenedy and Seguin. This memoir is addressed to her youngest son, Henry, born in 1907, who had apparently been urging her to "confess" about what had happened before he was born. McCallum also was responding to Henry's questions about his grandmother and his teasing accusation that his mother neglected him as the youngest child. She decided to keep the document, noting that "Our great-grandchildren would consider it *quite unique* and a real find."

Kathleen was *six weeks* old when we moved to *Kenedy*, Alvaro six months old when we left (July, 1900). *Kenedy* note[17] was known as a

[14] Boone, "Arthur Newell McCallum," 1, 3; *Handbook of Texas*, 2:37.

[15] Typescript, n.d., folder on JYM's marriage and death, McCP, II.

[16] Dates of birth for the McCallum children may be inferred from a variety of sources, but they are listed in Jane McCallum's hand in a black bound record book which also contains diary entries for 1939 and 1940, p. 184, in the possession of Betty Jane McCallum Ozbun.

[17] McCallum's note at the bottom of the first manuscript page calls attention to her error. Kathleen "was born July 23. We must have moved in August."

feudist town then. Six men had been killed about a year before our arrival. There seemed nothing for the inhabitants to do but *meet trains, get mad*, sit & gossip when not using their shooting irons. Dad [A. N. McCallum] had to keep the boys of one gang on one side of school at recess & his principal [kept] the boys of their foes on the other to avoid fights.

Dad complained of the lack of outside venetian blinds (not the type now in vogue) on the 8 room two-story school building, and of the need of a piano.

Out of a clear sky the idea came to me to kill two birds with one stone by putting on some plays ("establishing a little theatre" we would express it now). True I knew very little about it outside of having "taken parts," but no one else knew more, so why not? To think was to start. Among those I had the nerve to "train" I recall Mr. Bain (R.R. Agent & uncle of Jim Bain the present banker), Mr. Goff the hotel keeper, Miss Rosa Autry (later Mrs Will Nichols[)] the town belle. People were delighted with our performances, and we cleared enough with several plays to buy all the blinds needed, and also a good piano. Also, we furnished a *new topic of conversation* in fact, more than I had bargained for—the whisper went around that I had been *an actress!* I did not know whether to consider it a compliment or a slam. But it must have savored of the latter since friends ardently denied it but did not let it reach the shooting stage!

While making money for the schools [the] realization dawned that teachers obviously werent expected, except for nine months, to be as other people who eat, wear clothes and have shelter. "Charity might begin at home" I thought. So I organized an "elocution" class as we called it then, and also trained children in putting on little plays and charged tuition for same. (Henry, boy, I marvel at having the nerve when I knew so little about these things. No inferiority complex there—or—I just cannot account for it)

Get Dad to tell you how some of the rancher-farmers brought in chickens, others eggs, a turkey, a cured ham, and I'll never forget the half of a big porker one man brought in, in payment of tuition. Occasionally I'd receive cash, and boy, how proud Id be to help so much.

(Some day I'd like to write a story about ~~one of the~~ a finest women I ~~ever knew~~, Mrs. J. W. Rutledge—and she could *de-horn a cow* or nurse the sick with equal ease & efficiency. She seemed—no *was*, no "seeming" with her—very fond of me and was a great help to this "child."

She cut my half-hog into parts and showed me what to use & how to make sausage, lard, crackling-bread & how to pickle the two feet & make sauce out of the half head. She & her two girls were very fond of Sis [Kathleen] and helped me with her a lot.)

No, Mamma was not with me but with Papa [Alvaro Yelvington] whom she continued to be with until his death [in 1903] when Brown [the fourth child, born the same year] was a baby. I had my washing & ironing and floor scouring done, but no servant otherwise[.] The only problem with "Sis" I recall is when she got to be impatient about her food & would dash the first thing I gave her to the floor. I saw that unless curbed her impatience (or temper) would rule her and me too. So we had it out one day until I "conquered her," as the expression was and that was the last of her tantrums.

This account of life may sound dismal to you, but to me it was *fun, life, adventure* and the satisfying of an innate urge to—Well, what do you think? That Sis was neglected? Ask Dad.[18]

Seguin While I was delighted to move to the town where my Mother had grown up, and be associated with friends I'd had since early childhood, I soon realized that being so well known was indeed a handicap. Pretty women, pretty clothes[,] willow plumes, teas, card parties[,] receptions with hostesses vieing with one another on *decorations* and menu—just round and round and around again! I cut out the cards and Dad [eliminated] the dances right off, but I succumbed to more of the other than before or since, simply because I saw no way out.

I grasped at the Shakspere Club (and Mrs. Dibrell[19] who also was blessed (or cursed) with an urge to do what she could in return for the gift of life) as a drowning man at a straw.

We [—] rather she—the rest of us *helped* ... formed a *Village* Improvement Society (a few objected to the term "village"). I was chairman of the committee that persuaded property owners to plant all of those trees— too bad we chose hackberries—and then persuaded the city fathers to have them watered. Then we raised enough money to build two large club rooms with folding doors. One we met in & used as a library the other we furnished free with maid service to bedraggled, tired country women for their babies while they shopped Saturdays. I was astonished

[18] A first draft of the second page of this manuscript is entirely crossed out and labeled "skip." The information is identical to that in the alternate draft, except for the conclusion to the Kenedy section which states that without a full-time servant "Sis was the *first* child to be neglected, tho nobody ever guessed it. Enough queer things happened there [in Kenedy] to fill a small volume, but it was *fun* and *adventure* and life was young!"

[19] Ella Dibrell's husband was a state senator from 1894 to 1902 (*Handbook of Texas*, 1:500). She later became active in the woman suffrage movement. See JYM diary, Mar. 12, 1917, below and Part II, *n*50.

& gratified to receive that centennial book from the Seguin Chamber of Commerce last year with an inscription in recognition of all this.

No—*grandmother* [Mary Yelvington] was *still missing*! And I kept only one maid, so I guess Kathleen & Alvaro were both "neglected," tho happier, healthier, more loveable children I've not known. They had their sand piles and toys, a good fence around the yard, a big hall & bedrooms for play in the house, some grown person—the nurse or myself or some neighbors who loved to play with them, always within hearing. They tumbled in bed with us for a romp of mornings, and there were romps at night and I read to my children until—well ask Sis about this!

Artie [Arthur, Jr.] arrived in November [1901], before we left Seguin the next July a year. Mamma came to me then & I recall crying I was so glad to see her because Papa was so ill I feared she couldnt leave him to come & Artie was *so late* arriving [*i.e.*, being born].

LaVernia was just 19 miles across country from Seguin and some gorgeous day I'd say "Lets go see Grandma & Grandpa!" Kathleen & Alvaro would sit on the low seat of the phaeton, I'd drive and the maid would hold Artie & away we'd go!! We had a splendid horse, spirited Hamiltonian;[20] (if that means any-thing to automobile drivers) and I loved to drive him. Dad used to make me take a pistol (much to my amusement) because the road led through a Negro Colony. Such good times we'd have, and, looking back I cannot recall that the visits entailed any trouble. Of course, we remained only a part of two days, so didn't have to take much along. (Dad wasn't willing for us to be away longer)

When the Austin vacancy occurred I had a terrible time persuading Dad to apply—perhaps your inferiority complex comes in there—and had to call in assistance to get him off on the train to follow his application with a *personal appearance* before the board (Austin sch. Bd)

I was expecting Brown in the Fall (October [1903]) but that lovely cut-glass vase was given me by the valedictorian & salutatorian of Seguin High School (Hilmar Weinert was the former, do not recall [the] latter) for *teaching them how to say their speeches*, etc. Also I trained the performers for commencement night & was behind the scenes *prompting* them when the long distance call came & Dad was told he had been elected here Austin. Twas a dramatic moment! [illegible marginal comment] I have to confess further that I was president of the Shakspere Club & had taken quite a hand in having Mrs Dibrell made district president at the 5th district of Federated [Women's] Clubs meeting held in Seguin. In the mean time I

[20] She means Hambletonian, a well-known breed of trotting horses.

had managed to eliminate card (mostly euchre as bridge was just coming in) parties and a lot of society stuff

So you see, the "neglect" did not start with you. If I were able to be out of bed and rid of this terrible cold, I'm sure I could *confess* a lot more. *You were the only child* that received *too much* attention

Funny thing is, I am *an unregenerate sinner!!!* I know that I did not give one-third the time (if that much) to civic and cultural interests—we attended church regularly then too. (tho at heart I was never a Presbyterian—as the great majority of my friends gave to cards, dances, teas, receptions, planning beautiful clothes *et cetera*.[)][21]

The consequences of the McCallum family's move to Austin in 1903 were enormous both for the city's public schools and for Texas women. Jane McCallum supplied additional details of her husband's selection for the Austin post in a later note.

I cannot recall who first notified my husband of the impending need to secure a new superintendent for Austin's schools, but suspect the then board president, Judge Z. T. Fulmore. I *do distinctly* recall having—what I described in my write-and-run diary as—"a *terrible time*" persuading him to apply, and then to go to the Capitol City for a requested "appearance before the board." A dear friend and close neighbor, wife of our family physician, Dr. A. M. Stamps, and mother of Austin's Mrs. A. J. Wirtz,[22] if living, would testify that the two of us literally *pushed* Arthur on the Austin-bound train; for with all his ability to promote causes and other people, his energy and leadership, Arthur McCallum was no self-promoter—he was overly shy in that respect.

However, members of the Seguin school board and other residents had done some "promoting" for him:

On that eventful evening, June 5, 1903, while my husband was conducting graduation exercises in Seguin . . . , Austin trustees were cogitating the testimonials of thirty-four applicants for the job of running their schools.

Arthur's friends were said to have expediently reserved his for the last

---

[21] Untitled biographical note, folder on research notes and articles, McCP, II.

[22] The Stamps's daughter Kittie Mae married Wirtz in 1913. Wirtz's field of legal expertise included oil and gas law. He was an early promoter of Lyndon Johnson's political career, and served as undersecretary of the U.S. Department of the Interior for seventeen months in 1940 and 1941 (*Handbook of Texas*, 3:1122).

and to have started with the late Judge F. C. Weinert's statement that *"the* [Seguin] *Board has re-elected Professor* McCallum with an advanced salary!" The Judge had served his city on the school board, and Guadalupe County as judge and in both houses of the [state] legislature.[23]

Arthur McCallum was elected superintendent of Austin Public Schools by the board of trustees in 1903, a position he held until his retirement in 1942. The family of five relocated for the last time. Jane McCallum recalled their journey from Seguin in a poignant essay, probably written in the early 1920s. She provides some insights into her feelings about pregnancy and motherhood.

The essay reveals also that her view of blacks was no different from that of most white Texans at the time. Through a variety of means, the dominant culture sought to preserve the status of blacks as second-class citizens. The state constitution mandated separate (consequently inferior) schools for blacks. Primary election laws and the poll tax effectively disenfranchised them. Austin restaurants, churches, and other public facilities were segregated as rigidly in practice as the streetcars were by a 1906 city ordinance.[24] McCallum's patronizing attitude and her use of what seem now to be glaring stereotypes are not at all surprising given the pervasive atmosphere of the time.

NOBLESSE OBLIGE

I married at eighteen, and the first four of ~~my~~ our babies fairly tumbled into the world with less than two years intervening. . . .

Three months before the birth of our fourth child, [their father] accepted the position he continues to occupy - that of superintendent of schools in a large university town.

After his election, it became necessary for him to go at once to our new home. I was to follow with our seventeen-months old baby [Arthur, Jr.] and his faithful negro nurse Julie in about a week - the two older children were visiting their grand-parents.

[23] "I cannot recall . . . ," typescript, n.d., McCP, II. The text beginning with "Judge F. C. Weinert's statement" is taken from a handwritten revision of the last paragraph, McCP, II. The ellipsis deletes words referring to a missing portion of the document.

[24] Lewis L. Gould, *Progressives and Prohibitionists: Texas Democrats in the Wilson Era* (Austin, 1973), 48-49; Seymour V. Connor, *Texas: A History* (New York, 1971), 302; Brown, *Hood, Bonnet, and Little Brown Jug*, 149-50; David C. Humphrey, *Austin: An Illustrated History* (Northridge, Ca., 1985), 173.

Only five days had elapsed when my husband telephoned, begging me to "come on" the next day, as he was "so lonesome."

I promised. But when I told Julie, the nurse, she held up her hands in despair.

"Fer de Lawd's sake, Miss Jane," she protested, "Howze you gwine ter get dar in yo perdition, wid dat little imp? I kaint go kase I aint got a clean rag ter my back. I'se sent all my close ter de launry - jess like white folks - kase I got to look spunctious when I nusses dem chilluns in de city."

She spoke truly. So next morning "little Imp" - as bad, beautiful, darling and daring a baby boy as ever lived - and I set out on our half-day's journey, which entailed a change of trains and a tiresome wait in a crowded city depot.

Was I "stared at impudently," or made to feel "out of place," or "in disgrace?"

On the contrary, the only indication I had that I had been "stared at" sufficiently for my condition to be realized, was the wonderful consideration shown me.

The train had scarcely started when "little Imp" also started - for the open door. Before I could rise, three men I had never seen before were after him. From that time on, every man in the car seemed to look upon the baby as his personal charge, and "Imp" suited him; for he was on a regular "tear" - laughing, kicking, protesting, pulling at their hair, papers, watches, trying to escape through the door, and throwing one man's new Stetson nearly out of the window.

When he wore one group out, he was passed on to another, seemingly by some mutual though unspoken understanding.

Yet no embarrassing attention was shown me. Personally I was not made to feel that I was in any way "different" from other women travellers.

When the station where we changed trains was reached, an employee saw that I alighted safely.

A man took little "Imp" in his arms and courteously - almost reverently, I distinctly recall - asked me our destination; but after my reply he hurried away with the baby before I could even thank him.

I sat in a comparatively quiet part of the bustling station, and again received only normal attention, except that whenever baby dashed from my side there was immediately some one in pursuit.

This tactful care and consideration for approaching motherhood, continued to my destination, where baby's last self-appointed guardian handed him over - with great relief, I am sure - into the wide-spread arms of his waiting "da-da."

On account of a house shortage - even then - we were compelled to remain in a hotel for two weeks. We had a table reserved for us in as quiet a corner as could be found, and Julie, starched and immaculate, arrived to take charge of the baby. Men did not hesitate to come to our table and introduce themselves to their new city superintendent of schools and his wife, and to sit and talk with us.

A baby is a great exponent of democracy. Through ours I met the majority of the remaining men and women who frequented the hotel. When they said complimentary things about little "Imp," my husband and I would fairly trip each other's words in our joy at telling of the two older children expected to join us as soon as we could find a comfortable cottage to move into. Our listeners may have pitied us, 'tis true, but we saw only approval or downright envy in their smiling countenances.

Looking back . . . , I suppose I must have appeared very much like a child with her dolls. As soon as number four [Brown, with whom she had been pregnant during the 1903 journey] was old enough to be taken out in his buggy (and that was very soon, for he was the largest in the lot, fully as bright as the others, and now at seventeen weighs 182 pounds, and is six feet two inches tall), Julie and I took the greatest delight in "dressing up" all four and going on parade with them. It is true that often the first one dressed looked like a mud-pie by the time we reached the last, but youthful enthusiasm, perseverance and ingenuity are hand maidens: so, after a time "shining faces," glistening curls and immaculate little frocks would adorn all four at the same time, and we'd sally forth.

As with Tom Sawyer, onlookers may have envied us our employment because of our own evident enjoyment in it. I learn, as the years advance, that those things we prize most highly and openly come to assume value in the eyes of others.

Or it may have been just our happiness in the children, not the little ones themselves, that people envied and enjoyed. At any rate, such expressions as, "Oh, aren't they darling!" "How I'd love to steal them!" "What adorable children!" were sufficiently numerous to bring a grin to Julie's ebony face that half concealed it with a row of perfect, lustrous white teeth, and a smile to my own face that could not possibly have half revealed my pride in announcing to the world, as did the Roman matron of old, "These are *my* jewels!"

If any passed us without taking notice, we felt so sorry for them, feeling certain they were engrossed with some great sorrow or responsibility.

Four years passed before number five arrived [Henry in 1907]. The little lonely "only child" next door called to see the "new baby." As he left with his parents, he vociferously wailed, "If I'd a known the stork was goin' to bring a baby, I'd sure have beat those McCallum kids to it!"

And to us, his seemed typical of the attitude of the majority of our friends. . . .[25]

The family, which by the end of 1903 included four children, gave Jane McCallum much pleasure and absorbed most of her energies during her first decade in Austin. Yet she reserved some time for her own enjoyment. After doing extensive research on her ancestors, she applied for membership in the Colonial Dames and was accepted in the Texas chapter in 1905.[26] She had joined the quaintly spelled Austin Shakspere Club by 1906 and participated in a program which debated "The Wooings in Shakspere's plays: Are they natural?"[27]

In addition to her social and cultural pursuits and her children, her husband Arthur was a prime focus of Jane McCallum's life. While he was in Milwaukee in February 1905, no doubt tending to educators' business, she wrote him a letter which he failed to "destroy at once." Some of the closeness of their relationship is revealed in the details of their family routine.

Saturday 10 P.M.

My own Darling—

It is now past ten o'clock—the babies (including *Brown*) were fast asleep by 7:30 but Onie came over and remained until ten.

Did you know what happened at my end of the 'phone this afternoon? I tried *so* hard but *couldn't* hold out and was so afraid you'd know Id *broken down* for I nev[e]r did get out "good bye." I didn't cry long tho' for the babies discovered me and as you men sometimes observe—the best way to comfort a woman is to put her to comforting others. They didn't understand it at all and were nearly heart-broken. In their prayers they all added "take good care of papa and bring him safely home to us." I must go to bed now and finish my letter in the morning. I hope you are safely and soundly asleep by now and I know if you were here you'd be *sending me to bed* so good-night my precious Arthur.

    [25] JYM, "Noblesse Oblige," short stories folder, McCP, II. Material referring to a magazine article on the benefits of childlessness, to which this essay is a response, has been omitted.

    [26] Mary F. Gorwerman(?), Corresponding Secretary, Colonial Dames of America, to JYM, Nov. 2, 1905, Colonial Dames material, McCP, II.

    [27] Austin Shakspere Club, *1906-07 Yearbook*, folder on Shakspere Club, Box 8, McCP, II.

"Good Morning—have you used Pears soap?" I venture to say you've used *somebodys* or *know* the *reason why*!! I wish I could even hope that where you are the day is as glorious as it is here. Kathleen has gone to S.[unday] S.[chool] and the others are happy over the promise of a drive "out in the countwy" this after-noon. Mr Miller will be away from home so Mrs M is going with us and help "hold them down." You were the honored host (tho' absent) at an elaborate spread yesterday after-noon. Lillian and Robert were here so K.[athleen,] L.[illian] and Alvaro were appointed a committee on entertainment by Arthur[,] Brown and Robert and went to town and invested the four nickles in pop corn, zu zu's, marsh mallows and mixed candy and such a tea-party upon their return!!

We all slept together last night[,] and this morning Arthur not realizing his where abouts waked me saying "I wants to det in bed wiv you papa." K[athleen] cried for you and Alvaro said "Papa is staying away so long we cant wemember how he looks—make him come home mamma." We talked about you until time to get up. . . .

Daddy darling—*do get a gown* this *very day* and have your *trousers pressed* tonight. Mr Miller said you[r] over-coat was beautiful—I feel so well satisfied now with your appearances. Had you worn the other I would have felt worried every time I'd imagine your "seedy" looks in that coat. You didn't know it but I had it hidden away. Intended using *force* (not "Sunny Jims" however)

Alvaro is in bath tub and Brown assisting Bertha to bathe him much to A's disgust. Arthur is under the bed with the *seventh* member of the family and I *should* be in the kitchen. Will send this to the office. I'll have them (babies) affix their official *signatures* in their next—This is just from—

             "*Me*"
Destroy this *at once* and next time I'll sign it "*I*"—*may-be*
Oh, daddy I don't see how—nothing
I've been *baby* enough already haven't I?[28]
Don't fail to write *every day* and wire if you get sick even a little bit.
                          Lovingly
                             J[29]

[28] One interpretation of these two lines is that Jane McCallum started to write that she didn't see how she could manage things while he was away, or something similar, then chided herself for her dependency. She wrote later that the antics of her children "amused me so that Dad often remarked that he was bringing me up along with the rest of you. Poor Dad, I fear there was truth in this" (untitled biographical note, folder on research notes and articles, McCP, II).

[29] JYM to Arthur N. McCallum, [Feb. 26, 1905], folder of JYM letters to family, McCP, II. An incident involving an acquaintance is deleted by ellipses.

Even with four children, Jane McCallum kept busy writing a spelling text with her husband during their early years in Austin. The youngest of the clan, Henry, joined the family in October 1907. His mother later reminisced about the speller and Henry's childhood.

We wanted you to be a girl so badly that when I heard a neighbor say "pshaw!" on being told that you were a boy I resented it, and was a little on the defensive about you. But there was no need. The entire neighborhood (we all knew one another then) was foolish about you[.] I could write a pamphlet on this. You should be a good speller for the old lapboard you see around is the one I used before you were born to write the McCallum-Horn spelling book on. Dad got up the exercises, rules etc but naturally had no time to select the words. Mr. Horn's contribution was nil. But—here was a chance to augment our meagre salary—what about it? I couldn't spell so well, I'd never taught a day in my life, but I'd loved and observed children and had groups around me from Kenedy through Seguin & Austin. I did not have an idea how to proceed, but "Brother Rabbit he bleeged to climb dat tree."[30] Believe it or not, I went entirely through a dictionary *seven* (or eight I forget) times. Each time I selected words for a grade, beginning at first, and ran a mark through it. Tedious? Just try it! Of course I expect a doctor would have forbidden this—but I tried to make up on exercises with children etc[.] Anyway the book was adopted for first a *six year* followed by a *five year* term! And thats that. Twas a *bread* saver!

After your arrival I someway, somehow had my hands pretty full at home with sewing, yard, one maid, no horse (he'd eaten green cane & died) this big house & keeping up the minimum of social obligations—Shakspere Club, Colonial Dames (twice a year but they frequently drafted me as toastmistress), University club occasionally (At the close of our first 2 years here we[']d been invited to join 25 organizations including several ladies Aid [(]I laughed inside with thought *I* was lady needing aid[)] & Missionary Societies, the U.T. Town & Gown & Country Clubs). Couldn't afford to. I was daffy about our new home built 190[7?] & my flowers (never washed dishes in my life without thinking "Any Negro could do this, why don't I use my brains (if any) & make money to *hire* one. I had—'nother confession—a complex on not doing my share—on being a *barnacle* in the world. And how I resented "influenc-

[30] This is McCallum's Uncle Remus manner of saying that she had no choice in the matter, but simply had to forge ahead.

ing" a yard man or charcoal burner on his vote while *I* was politically classified with "Idiots, imbeciles & the Insane") . . .[31]

Back to you. I never saw a child more adored by everyone. Neighbors would telephone for you, send for you. Alvaro's dog objected to being carried around by the collar & stub tail by you so we got another that would submit to your treatment. The older children spoiled you, we did too—*everybody* did. But how could we help it when you were so sweet & affectionate? Leslie Clancy, Margaret Miller[32]—"Mooney" (your name for her) Harper were jealous about you. . . .[33]

Jane Y. McCallum enrolled at the University of Texas for the fall semester in 1912. She was not concerned about earning a degree, but registered for classes in English composition and journalism which, presumably, she felt would be useful to her. She continued taking courses through the spring of 1915.[34]

Her children provided much of the material for the themes she wrote as a student, several of which survive. The "Mary" of one story is based primarily on the experiences of Kathleen, who, in the fall of 1913, had gone to Sweet Briar College in Virginia.[35] The hero of the story below is doubtless one of her sons. Although the quality of this early prose is very uneven, one can see McCallum's compassion for her children and the depth of her understanding of them at various ages.

A LITTLE PILGRIM

It was but yesterday that with cap thrust back, hands in pockets, trouser legs dangling, and lips puckered in a laborious effort to whistle, he loitered on the sun-kissed path that leads from Babyville to Boyville. The elves of the swimming hole and the magic of the woods called to his

[31] According to Article VI of the Constitution of 1876, those excluded from voting were persons under twenty-one years of age, idiots and lunatics, paupers, convicted felons, and U.S. servicemen. "Every male person subject to none of the foregoing disqualifications" could vote, provided he met residence requirements and, for aliens, declared his intention to become a U.S. citizen (John Sayles, *The Constitutions of the State of Texas* . . . [St. Louis, 1888], 550-51). Women were therefore limited, as McCallum points out, to offering political advice to the men of their acquaintance, including hired hands and tradesmen.

[32] Leslie Clancy, residing at 504 West 31½ Street, became a school teacher. Margaret Miller lived at 3200 Guadalupe (*Directory of the City of Austin: 1912-1913* [Houston, 1912], 101, 219).

[33] Untitled biographical note, folder on research notes and articles, McCP, II.

[34] Editor's telephone conversation with University of Texas Registrar's Office, Feb. 24, 1986.

[35] JYM, "Mary," short stories folder, McCP, II.

instincts primeval, and in his heart there thrilled an answering echo. But, in the very midst of his ecstasy, the roguish expression vanished; the brown eyes widened in babyish bewilderment; the lips quivered; and a yearning backward glance was given to the fast receding, beautiful land of fairies, dreams, and "counterpane."

But backward glances are not characteristic of childhood days. A chubby fist brushed away the momentary tear; he called to his dog; shied a rock at an unoffending tree; and plunged on—deep into the delights of the land of Boyville. . . .

It seemed only a twinkling and the baby had vanished utterly; and in his place a "Barefoot boy with cheeks of tan" unblushingly declared his preference for the woods to the yard, the barn to the house, the *Forty Thieves* to *First Steps For Little Feet*, and "mud hole" to the carefully enameled bath tub.

But his instincts did not become wholly savage as many members of the purblind race of grown-ups would have us believe is the natural state of boys at this transitional age. No doubt, to the observer of mere externals, appearances—and sounds—were often against him; but who ever heard of a full-blooded little savage marching home from a day in the woods, tired but happy and triumphant in the knowledge that he had rescued from a watery grave, and was bearing to the warmth of his own fireside, five half-starved, two-thirds drowned, long-eared, yellow hound puppies? Their state of shivering dampness had so appealed to his higher nature that he had tucked them away on the inside of his blouse, and folded them close to his heart. On another occasion, the boy's dogs, incited by their young masters, had killed two mother possums. Thirteen babies were found; and the effect was surprising—to speak lightly—when our little Pilgrim and two companions appeared with all of the thirteen perched on their heads and shoulders, and swinging, possum-fashion, from their fingers. Their purpose was to rear them.

School days held many sorrows for the boy; for while he droned over reading, writing, and arithmetic, his thoughts were far away with his beloved dogs, chasing over hills and brakes, mountains and deep ravines. And then, so many wholly senseless and unreasonable demands were made. It was evidently a crisis calling for the exertion of all his pent up ingenuity—and he rose to the occasion. His expression was wickedly impish when, one morning, the usual inspection of finger nails disclosed the fact that these frequently offending appendages were carefully, if not artistically, discolored with the stain of green pecans. He relieved his overburdened shoulders of another unnecessary responsibility by wheedling a barber into shaving a natural part in his hair; but before

appearing in the bosom of his family with this latest evidence of his
budding genius, he had thoughtfully padded his trousers most carefully.

Constantly engaged in similar occupations—which cause him to be at
once a torment and a delight—he journeys on, "and the clatter and clash
and hubbub that attends the triumphs of the kingdoms of the earth pass
by unconquered Boyville as the shadow of a dream."[36]

The young woman named Grace in McCallum's story of a "A Day at
Bull Creek" possesses much of her own enthusiasm and love of the
outdoors. Automobile drives in the Hill Country, outings on Lake
Austin, picnics, hikes to Mt. Bonnell, and occasional camping vaca-
tions were always a delightful respite for McCallum. The narrative,
excerpted here, is burdened by McCallum's disregard for paragraphing and her predilection for complex sentences heavily laced with
semicolons, but the meaning could hardly be more clear. Like Grace,
McCallum relished action and the satisfaction of conquering the
highest peak.

A DAY AT BULL CREEK

It was hardly seven o'clock, but the rumble of a long wagonette, the
clatter of horses' hoofs, and the merry laughter of twenty young voices
announced that the picnickers had arrived; and Grace, who had been
awaiting them with some impatience, quickly climbed the steps at the
back of the conveyance, and returning greetings, made her way between
the long double row of "shining morning faces" until she reached the
only remaining vacant seat. A signal was given; the driver—perched
high in front—cracked his whip over the backs of the four sleek bays, and
the start was made for a day at Bull Creek.

Grace had long since discovered that she is a victim of "wood-magic,"
and therefore was not surprised at her "exuberance of feeling" as the
party penetrated deep into the woods—which were still sparkling with
the early morning dew, and alive with the carolling of feathered song-
sters—and emerged to catch a glimpse of the drowsy, shimmering river,
reluctantly bidding farewell to the heart of the misty mountains. The
driver's ringing command, "All out 'till we get over some of these hills,"
was received joyously. Grace was first to touch the ground, and last to
clamber in again at the call, "All aboard!" . . .

* JYM, "A Little Pilgrim," short stories folder, McCP, II. Ellipses replace a poem which
McCallum quoted.

[When they had chosen a spot and eaten their picnic lunch,] Grace gave one gleeful little whoop, and was away to revel in the glories of mountain and stream. After racing up the road, gathering cat-claw and wreathing garlands of wild clematis, she led her companions to a perfect little lake that is enclosed by a trickling waterfall on one side, and by huge rocks on the other. It looked deep and dangerous, but she soon found a girl who was willing to try it with her; and, dressing in their suspiciously convenient bathing suits, they plunged in. They bruised themselves against hidden rocks, stepped suddenly into water over their heads, and came up splashing and spluttering; but their delight was so evident that others soon joined them. All aglow and tingling after their plunge, Grace and two companions decided to scale the cliff. The path grew gradually narrower as it neared the summit until they finally stood on a ledge not more than a foot wide; and here they clung to the cliff, and laughed in impish glee at the fright they caused all who saw them. However, the path had curved away before reaching the summit, and Grace was determined to see "beyond the Alps." Returning, she found a fresh recruit, and they decided to climb the highest mountain. Their time was limited; so they went as nearly straight up as was possible. They slipped on the fallen cedar, and fell headlong; clung to rotten branches that gave way, and caused them to fall back; riddled their shoes and bruised their feet on the sharp pieces of stone; and scratched their arms pushing through the dense chaparral. But they reached the very highest point of the mountain—saw the world beyond; and surely Italy could not have seemed fairer to the Alpine climber.

As Grace—with scarred shoes, torn clothes, flying hair, and blistered face—walked serenely into camp, Lucy, with an I-feel-sorry-for-you air, remarked, "My, what a sight you are. I spent such a happy and profitable day. . . . I've finished this garment—embroidered steadily for three hours—while I listened to Alice read *Hamlet*, parallel reading for this term you know."[37]

This final selection from about 1913 is the most obviously autobiographical. McCallum dramatizes the diversity in her day's engagements. Her emphatic handwritten comment upon rereading it was, "*Dull sez I* 40 years later—Dec. 1943."[38] The style is loose and wordy. Yet the acute observations scattered throughout give it life.

[37] JYM, "A Day at Bull Creek," short stories folder, McCP, II.
[38] Either arithmetic was not one of McCallum's strengths or she misdated the note by ten years. Although undated, this theme could not have been written in 1903.

FROM AN ENGLISH 3 CLASS TO A
COLONIAL DAME LUNCHEON

The trouble began when I started to dress. Class is not over until eleven-thirty, and, as I was due at the Driskill[39] at eleven, it suddenly occurred to me that there would be no time after class in which to return home and array myself in the attire considered essential to proper participation in a Colonial Dame function. Naturally, the said attire would be highly improper for attendance at a morning university class. Anyway, this particular class is an unusually normal, candid aggregation; with the sex who proverbially profess contempt for overdressed women, greatly predominating.

The class is very large, and many types are represented. We have one or more members of the pedantic school; also, we have the very proper person, who, like a certain locally famous English professor, would probably refuse to receive an express package if the address were improperly punctuated. Then, there is the school boy (or girl) type, who, when he is, on rare occasions, familiar with the text, wishes to recite it all. Representatives of the wholly serious-minded, gravely inquire, after one of Lamb's most deliciously humorous passages, "Now do you suppose he really meant that?" I have not touched on the foibles of the would-be-come-back type; for that is nearing home.... [T]he airing of these diverse peculiarities, but lends variety and a certain interest to the class work; for our instructor never allows the expression of opinions to the extent of tediousness. He is uniformly polite; but when a student has consumed enough time, or, is failing to talk interestingly, or to the point, Dr. C- can look into space, slightly open his lips, and assume the most discouragingly vacant expression that it has ever been my lot to look upon. The desired effect is generally instantaneous.

But, as a class, I've never seen a healthier, more wholesome lot. If mistakes are made, a hearty laugh is likely to greet it (and who does not prefer this to the quiet nudging, or whispered sarcasm?); if something good is said, the approval is equally free and hearty. Criticism is given and taken in perfect good humor; and, when there is cause for a bit of merriment, instructor and class enjoy it mutually.

Now imagine appearing before this class in the raiment suitable for a grand-dame function! Verily a compromise was a pressing necessity; so out of deference to the class instincts, I donned my best school dress; and,

---

[39] Still one of Austin's finest hotels, the Driskill is centrally located just off Congress Avenue. It was a fashionable meeting place for a variety of groups.

out of deference to the luncheon, placed a large American Beauty rose at my girdle. But a hat (the little trouble makers!) was a necessary adjunct to the costume. My school hat plainly would not do. I tried on my best hat, but couldn't muster the courage to wear it. Time was passing, and, in desperation, I tried a hat of last winter.... The car was coming; I grasped the things nearest, and stuffed them into the crown of my hat so that it would remain in place. ~~Among the articles thus used was a pair of torn kid gloves.~~ However, I walked into class with a rather self-satisfied feeling that my efforts at a compromise had not been in vain.

But my delusion was of short duration; for, as I looked around my side of the classroom, broad grins greeted me, or, more properly speaking, my hat. I was feeling sufficiently subdued, it seemed to me, when our instructor arrived; called the roll; and, after one glance of mild surprise, announced that we should, first of all, write an essay; "and," he added, ["]I suggest that one *on hats* would be suitable." I survived the hour, finding recompense in the thought that, perhaps, after all, the hat was "flossy" enough for the luncheon.

When I reached the Driskill, the business meeting which always precedes these semi-annual affairs, was well under way. I stood outside the door for a few moments, unobserved myself, but observing the scene within, and trying to adjust my contemplations to the changed atmosphere. My first thought was of the ... [live] illustrations of the essays on hats. I learned afterward that several of the ladies present had—during the past season—shortened their trips abroad that they might land before the law allowing "those horrid customs Inspectors" to confiscate their fine feathers went into effect. Perhaps, by so doing, they missed a visit to the Louvre, a trip up the Rhine, or an excursion into the Swiss mountains. But what if these pleasures were forborne; aren't they able to bear aloft trophies [the feathers] of their chase through foreign millinery shops— which excite the envy of all woman-kind?

My inspection over, I quietly slipped in and sat in the extreme rear. It was pleasant to feel young—by comparison—again. The majority of the Dames have attained the dignity, poise, and, alas, the avoirdupois, of forty summers; a great many have passed the three-score stage; and one dear little lady is past three-score and ten. Our president, tall and stately, dressed in dark silken garments—relieved by real, old lace,—and crowned with silvery hair, presided in a typically easy old-fashioned manner. It seemed as tho' I had entered a new world. The buzz and hurry of life, the clatter and clang of the streets and cars, seemed far removed. Here, people with unlimited time, sat and listened to each other with so much interest and repose that the occasional opening of an ivory fan, or the adjustment of a jeweled lorgnette, occasioned the only audible sounds.

The matters discussed at this business meeting concerned, chiefly, the finding and collecting of antiquities; the awarding of prizes to pupils in order to revive interest in colonial days and ways; and the heroic deeds of ancestors long since gone to their reward. Our dear little three-score-and-ten Dame, small of statu[r]e, but great in dignity, talked of her dear departed until the *noblesse oblige* of the fair assemblage was thoroughly tested. When she ceased speaking, the applause was just a trifle prolonged to have been wholly complimentary. But the dim eyes brightened; the expression of earnestness and sweet reserve relaxed into a proud smile. She rose and bowed;—and, with quavering voice, claimed our attention for another fifteen minutes, while she told of the inscriptions on the moss-covered tombstones of the old and ruined churchyard in which her remote ancestors lie buried.

When, at last, all conversation ceased, and the company seemed lost in reveries of the past, the President gently reminded us that the luncheon awaited our pleasure. With due dignity and ceremony,—nodding of aigrettes, trailing of skirts; and flashing of both jewels and wit, we escorted the visiting Dames,—here in attendance from many sections of the state,—to the "Ladies' Auxiliary;" where all "went merry as a marriage bell. . . ."[40]

Jane McCallum's earliest published work, "The Builder of Formosa," appeared in a University of Texas student literary magazine in 1915. The essay recalls her acquaintance with Austin sculptress (and woman suffrage advocate) Elisabet Ney, whom she visited from time to time at her unusual home and studio named Formosa. McCallum must have been encouraged to pursue her writing after winning the Fine Arts League prize in 1915 with this essay. The paragraph below evokes the atmosphere of Formosa, now the Elisabet Ney Museum.[41]

With its quaint, grey tower, miniature battlements, and old-world look, it lies removed from the noisy streets, amid a graceful wildness of

[40] JYM, "From an English 3 Class to a Colonial Dame Luncheon," short stories folder, McCP, II. Ellipses mark the omission of obscure details and McCallum's admission that the essay was unfinished.

[41] German-born and educated in Europe, sculptress Elisabet Ney moved to Austin in 1892, where she resided until her death in 1907. The Elisabet Ney Museum is located on 34th Street in Hyde Park (Humphrey, *Austin*, 145-47; Editor's interview with Fritz

flower and shrub, on a simple breadth of ground which falls gently away to a lake in the rear. The place is approached by a blue-bonnet bordered roadway, and immediately upon opening the gate, one feels as if he were suddenly stepping into another world. A mysterious little tinkle sounds from overhead—the magic signal to summon the haunting memories with which studio and garden are fraught; memories of by-gone days; of old-world associations; of youthful dreams come true; and yes, of the ghosts of Utopian dreams.[42]

   In addition to becoming a published author in the fall of 1915, when this essay appeared, Jane McCallum had also won election to the presidency of Austin's woman suffrage society. Her social conscience had discovered a constructive outlet that would occupy her—often more intensely than she might have wished—for the next three and a half years.

McCallum, Frances McCallum, and Janet Poage, Mar. 5, 1986); JYM, "The Builder of Formosa," *The Texas Magazine*, 31 [Oct. 1915]: 17-19).
   [42] JYM, "Builder of Formosa," 17.

Jane Y. McCallum liked to tell an anecdote from her early days as a lobbyist for woman suffrage. She had called a legislator out to speak with him.

He: Young woman, what are you doing meddling with men's affairs? You ought to be getting married.

She: I am already married.

He: You should be having children.

She: What is the limit? I already have five.

He: You ought to be home taking care of them.

She: They are all in school, besides they have a lovely grandmother at home, and if anything should happen to them, I would be notified immediately.

He: Then you should be home darning their stockings.

[Anecdote adapted from "Program of Suffrage Luncheon," March 26, 1930, p. 2, Series BB, McCallum Papers, Part I, Austin History Center.]

FAMILY ALBUM

Mary LeGette Yelvington, Jane Y. McCallum's "Mamma," married in 1874 at about age 20. Jane was born four years later. *(Courtesy, Austin History Center, Austin Public Library.)*

As a young girl, Jane LeGette Yelvington was "Janie" to her friends. (*Courtesy, Betty Jane McCallum Ozbun.*)

This photograph of Jane Yelvington dates from about the time of her marriage to Arthur Newell McCallum in 1896, when she was nearly 18. (*Courtesy, Betty Jane McCallum Ozbun.*)

Jane McCallum's notation on the reverse of a companion photograph states that this 1901 image was "taken when in New B[raunfels]" while her husband "was conducting a summer normal school. Artie was due in November." *(Courtesy, Austin History Center, Austin Public Library.)*

"Shining faces, glistening curls and immaculate little frocks" were required of Kathleen and Alvaro, the two oldest McCallum children, at this sitting about 1901. *(Courtesy, Betty Jane McCallum Ozbun.)*

From time to time Jane McCallum called on sculptress Elizabeth Ney at Formosa, Ney's home and studio on East 45th Street, where this photograph of McCallum was taken about 1905. *(Courtesy, Betty Jane McCallum Ozbun.)*

The family's home on West 32nd Street, which Jane McCallum designed in 1907, was granted historic zoning by the Austin City Council in 1986.

Henry, the youngest McCallum, and his nurse seem delighted with one of their home's spacious porches in this photograph from about 1910. *(Courtesy, Austin History Center, Austin Public Library.)*

This pair of studio portraits of Jane Y. and Arthur N. McCallum dates from about 1910, when they had lived in Austin for seven years. *(Courtesy, Austin History Center, Austin Public Library.)*

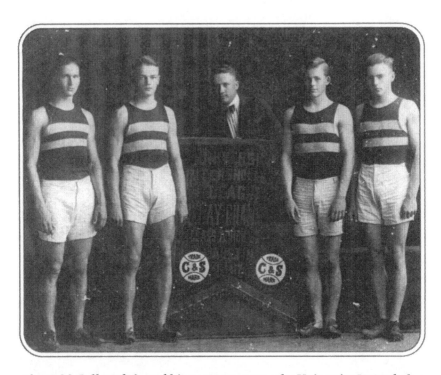

Alvaro McCallum, left, and his teammates won the University Interscholas-
tic League Relay for Austin High School in 1917. His mother referred to the
competition in her diary entry for May 11, 1917. *(Courtesy, Betty Jane Mc-
Callum Ozbun.)*

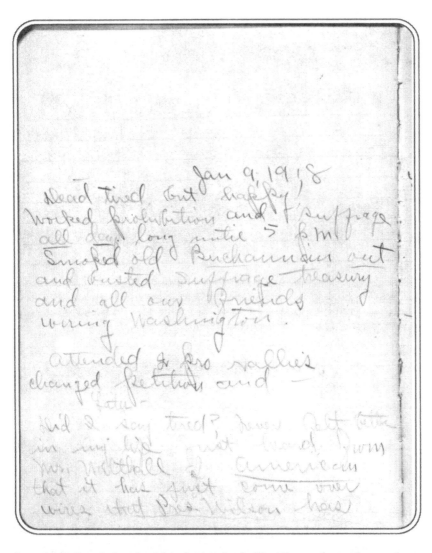

Jane McCallum's handwriting is unmistakable. The underscoring and ex-
clamation points clearly express her enthusiasm in this typical page from
her 1916-1918 diary. *(Courtesy, Austin History Center, Austin Public Library.)*

These proud women were the early birds on June 26, 1918: those who at 8 A.M. were waiting at the Travis County Court House to register to vote. Jane McCallum holds the figured bag near the center of the first row. *(Courtesy, Austin History Center, Austin Public Library. PICA11669)*

Governor William P. Hobby signed the full suffrage bill on February 5, 1919. The referendum on this constitutional amendment was set for May 24. *(Courtesy, Austin History Center, Austin Public Library. PICA11670)*

Kathleen McCallum, left, and Zatella Field taught in the same school in Pearsall, Texas, in 1919. *(Courtesy, Austin History Center, Austin Public Library.)*

The younger generation of McCallums gathered for this photograph in the 1920s. They are, from left to right, Alvaro, Kathleen, Henry, Alvaro's wife Melba, Brown, Fritz, and her husband Arthur, Jr. *(Courtesy, Betty Jane McCallum Ozbun.)*

PART 2

WAGING CAMPAIGNS

As early as 1903, Jane Y. McCallum refers to keeping a "write-and-run" diary.[1] This phrase accurately describes the one for the period of October 1916 through July 1918, the earliest diary extant.[2] When she had the time, McCallum recorded events both trivial and momentous in a breezy, informal style. She noted her reactions to her own and her family's activities and expressed opinions on incidents and people swirling about her.

The 1916-1918 diary was written in an old composition notebook which McCallum appropriated when her son Henry had finished with it. For the most part, the handwriting is quite legible. In her later years she clearly reread the diary, adding occasional explanatory notes. That several pages have been torn out, including at least some manuscript material, raises the natural but unanswerable questions, "who did it?" and "what have we lost?"

One suspects that McCallum may have been consciously writing for an audience that extended beyond her children. There are hints that upon rereading the diary, she recognized its value. She seems to have sought deliberately to compose a journal that accurately represented her life. (See the entry for May 11, 1917, below.)

By 1916, when the diary begins, the McCallum family had been living in their large home at 507 West 32nd Street for about eight years. Mary Yelvington, Jane's "Mamma," had joined them several years earlier[3] and regularly helped with the chores. The household often included a domestic employee whose duties entailed cooking, caring for the children, and otherwise lending a hand. The ages of the five children in 1916 ranged from nine-year-old Henry to University of

[1]JYM, "I cannot recall . . . ," typescript, n.d., McCallum Papers, Part II, Austin History Center, Austin Public Library (hereafter cited as McCP, II).

[2]JYM, Diary of Oct. 13, 1916-July 20, 1918, Series A.2, McCallum Papers, Part I, Austin History Center, Austin Public Library (hereafter cited as McCP, I).

[3]1912-1913 *Austin City Directory*, 327.

Texas student Kathleen. Alvaro and Arthur, Jr., were in their third year of high school, and Brown was an adolescent of thirteen. Arthur, Sr., aged fifty-one, was in his thirteenth year as Austin school superintendent, by which time he had succeeded in upgrading nearly every facet of the city's public education. He had convinced voters to support a bond issue for new school buildings, introduced innovations in curricula, established a free night school for adults, and created a separate division with a specially tailored program for junior high students.[4]

Her family's comings and goings figure prominently in Jane McCallum's diary for 1916-1918. But they share pages with several other themes which alternately claimed her attention and time: woman suffrage, World War I, and the controversy between the University of Texas and Governor James Ferguson.

When McCallum joined the Austin Woman Suffrage Association, she added to her already full schedule of mothering her children, participating in a variety of women's clubs, and attending university classes. It is not clear why she joined the Austin Woman Suffrage Association precisely when she did: on October 20, 1914.[5] She was perceptive enough to sense the injustice of being denied the ballot and clearly bright enough to imagine that her actions might make a difference. Perhaps the Colonial Dames and Shakspere Club were becoming a bit stale after her active memberships of nearly ten years in each. And perhaps she realized that she was approaching the last of the university courses she wished to take.

McCallum's enlistment in the suffrage cause coincided with its strong comeback in Texas. The state woman suffrage organization had been dormant since 1905.[6] The Texas Equal Rights Association had advanced the cause between 1893 and 1895 under the presidency of Rebecca Henry Hayes of Galveston.[7] The group ceased to function after Hayes opposed a lecture tour by Susan B. Anthony and did not retain the leadership. In 1903 the state's first enduring local suffrage group had organized in Houston, largely due to the talent and industry

[4]Boone, "Arthur Newell McCallum," 5-8, 10.
[5]Meeting of Oct. 20, 1914, Minute Book of the Austin Woman Suffrage Association (AWSA), 1908-1914, Barker Texas History Center, University of Texas at Austin (hereafter cited as BTHC).
[6]The discussion in this and the next two paragraphs is taken primarily from Nieuwenhuizen, "Minnie Fisher Cunningham and Jane Y. McCallum," 6-9, and A. Elizabeth Taylor, "The Woman Suffrage Movement in Texas," Journal of Southern History, 17 (May 1951): 196-204.
[7]During the 1890s, local suffrage societies were established in Denison, Taylor, Granger, Dallas, Fort Worth, Belton, and San Antonio as chapters of the Texas Equal Rights Association. See Taylor, "Woman Suffrage Movement in Texas," 197.

of Annette Finnigan and her two sisters. A Galveston chapter soon followed. These two groups composed the entire state association which first convened in December 1903. The crusade faltered before long when other cities ignored it, and the absence of the Finnigans from the state after 1905 left it moribund.

Between 1905 and 1912, the only bright note in the Texas suffrage movement occurred in Austin. Awakened by a lecture given by Dr. Anna Howard Shaw, president of the National American Woman Suffrage Association, capital city women established a suffrage club in 1908. Compared to women in other Texas cities, they may have been more attuned to the fine points of politics because of the legislature's proximity, and some no doubt had friendships with state government officials and employees. Regardless of the factors that precipitated its founding, the Austin group was strong enough to survive the state-wide indifference of the next few years.

The resurgence of the woman suffrage movement in Texas began in 1912. In that year, Eleanor Brackenridge of San Antonio roused enough members for a chapter in that city. Suffrage organizations soon sprouted in other towns. After a lapse of nine years, the state association convened in 1913, drawing representatives from seven cities. Annette Finnigan's return to Texas and active work for woman suffrage insured the continued vitality of the state group.

When Jane McCallum joined the Austin Woman Suffrage Association in 1914, the group counted more than seventy-five members. She was elected its president a year later.[8] At some point she jotted down some notes on what she "laughingly called" her "last day of freedom" just before being elected to the post. She had been hiking on Mt. Bonnell with her children, while Arthur remained at home with some friends.

When [I] returned Dad told me of [a] visit from Mrs. Dave Doom— "Nell"[9]—and Mrs. Bob Connerly—"Miss Lou" & the exciting news that they wanted to draft me for the presidency of the Austin woman suffrage (later called *equal* suffrage) association.

Dad knew how I felt about it all. [He] Told them to come again[.] . . .

[8]Meeting of Oct. 22, 1915, Minute Book of the AWSA, Dec. 14, 1915-May 8, 1916, Series C, McCP, I.

[9]Nell Doom was a lifelong friend of Jane McCallum and a co-worker on many committees and projects. In addition to her work for suffrage, she was later active in the Austin Woman's Club, Federated Women's Club of Austin, and United Daughters of the Confederacy (*Austin American*, Mar. 15, 1948, p. 9).

On [their] 2nd visit [they] told me of Dr. Margaret Hollidays dictum ("None but pretty women" etc) to start anew—etc[.]

Recall 1st surprise—they . . . thought all well and secure for my election without opposition[.] When [we] met in old Driskill Hotel[,] lo and behold a dark horse candidate appeared—good looking too,—wife of U.T. prof and looked like close [competitor].

I'll always remember Nell's (et al) *relief* when [they] told me frankly about it and asked so *anxiously* "but you *will* run wont you?" and my answer "Well you dont think I am a *quitter* do you?"

Then a little thing seemingly[,] but one of the *hardest* things I ever did. Several admonished me "You *must* vote (secret ballot) for yourself." [I answered,] "Oh, no—I cannot do that! I[']ll just turn in a blank." Their arguments overcame my qualms—I *couldn't* because of *our side* losing because of code. *I did* and we won.[10]

McCallum's duties as president of the Austin Woman Suffrage Association must have required some skill and perseverance, as the cause was not a particularly popular one with the general public. During the first year of her tenure, the organization conducted a door-to-door canvass of the city, seeking to win converts. A well-attended luncheon featured a speech by Austin Mayor A. P. Wooldridge and a suffrage song to the tune of "Tipperary." To raise funds, the group held a play and dance.[11]

At the May 1916 convention of the state suffrage society, which McCallum attended as a delegate,[12] the group took steps to expand its political influence. Members approved a plan to organize according to state senatorial districts and adopted a new name, Texas Equal Suffrage Association. Minnie Fisher Cunningham was reelected president.[13]

Fresh from their own meetings, the women lobbied the Texas Democratic Convention delegates later in May, seeking support for suffrage. Both there and at the Democratic National Convention in August, Governor James Ferguson aroused their ire by stating his unalterable opposition to their cause.[14]

[10]Quotations in the paragraph preceding the anecdote and the anecdote are from JYM, "Nell & Others," McCP, II. Ellipses replace two obscure references.

[11]AWSA Minute Book, 1915-1916, *passim*, Series C, McCP, I; *Austin American*, Mar. 14, 1916, p. 6.

[12]Meeting of Apr. 18, 1916, AWSA Minute Book, 1915-1916, Series C, McCP, I.

[13]Nieuwenhuizen, "Minnie Fisher Cunningham and Jane Y. McCallum," 26.

[14]Ibid., 17.

A year later Jane McCallum would compare the Ferguson administration—"would-be Kaiserism at home"—to "Kaiserism abroad."[15]
In the fall of 1916, however, the war in Europe seemed very remote.
Although hundreds of thousands of lives had been lost, only a handful
were American. Other than providing a constant source of conversation, the war had had a minimal impact on ordinary Austinites. The
following spring, when the United States entered the conflict, Jane
McCallum would record in her diary the heartache and personal
sacrifice it brought.

The actors are now all in place for the drama which began in the fall
of 1916. Members of the McCallum family were caught up in a host of
activities. World War I appeared in the background as a distant threat.
Texas suffragists commanded notice and already had reason to raise
their voices against the governor. When he embroiled the University of
Texas in controversy, Jane McCallum was ready to take a stand.

DIARY OF JYM

"— the branches of a tree
Spread no wider than its roots
And how shall the soul of a man
Be larger than the life he has lived?"[16]

"These sudden flashes in your soul,
Like lambent lightning on snowy clouds

Beware of the man who rises to power
From one suspender

Friday October 13, 1916

Never got up until 6.30 as today is circus day—consequently a
holiday. Had breakfast here and there all morning as Arthur & Brown
slept with James Rice *on his lawn* so they could go early to see the circus
unload, and they came straggling in. Then, since he is to play full-back on
Austin High against Gidding's High this afternoon, Alvaro was allowed

---

[15]JYM diary, June 15, 1917, Series A.2, McCP, I.
[16]The source of the first two epigraphs is Edgar Lee Masters's *Spoon River Anthology,*
initially published in 1915. Samuel Gardner, the greenhouse keeper, says now that he is
"an under-tenant of the earth," he knows that "the branches of a tree/ Spread no wider
than its roots." To Faith Matheny, the "sudden flashes in your soul" are almost mystical
experiences in which you catch "a little whiff of the ether/ Reserved for God Himself"
(Edgar Lee Masters, *Spoon River Anthology* [New York, 1962], 250, 255).

to sleep late—so did Kathleen. Read paper after breakfast[,] got Henry off to parade, Mr. M[cCallum] off to office, then spent two hours mending and adjusting Alvaro's foot-ball togs. *Sweaty* and dirty to be sure—queer how you don't mind if it is *off of your own boy*—(the sweat and dirt).

Then Ida washed my hair and it was time for A[lvaro][17] to come home for his togs and lunch if he was to get off in time. All sorts of 'phoning and excitement[,] then a hurry up, S.O.S. or what you may call from A. to pack his things in suit case and send [them] down by one of [the] boys—boys *all gone.* ~~Ida~~ Mamma & I finally stuffed the things in and got it off on street car—Hope the spikes in his shoes don't punch all the darned holes over again!

Sat. Oct. 13 [18]
2.30 P.M.

Was interrupted by Mr. M. and Henry coming from office where, according to custom, they had circus day lunch. Usually he has all the children with him, but K[athleen]'s outgrown it, Alvaro was away, Arthur arrived late; so only "Dad," Brown, and H.[enry] enjoyed the spread. Mr. M. had an afternoon at home—first—except Sundays—in many moons.

Brown, Wroe Alexander, and Jack Straus donned hunting coats, canteens[,] guns, blankets and food and left for the woods at about eight last night. Mighty Nimrods! Wish they'd come on home—would feel safer about the guns. Kip went too.

I've always wanted a *"plunging full-back,"* (not quarter back, center, or half back) and I guess my wish has come to pass from this clipping.[19] Bless his heart, he was sleepy and sore when he arrived from Giddings at 7.30 after an all night *sit up.* Mr. Gullet 'phoned at 11 to have him go to San Marcos with him to watch a game there. Hope he doesn't snore loud enough to raise a disturbance.

Brown just arrived with *"fo*[ur] *ducks"* he is calling.

Went to Dr. Holliday[20] to be "done up" this A.M. Afterward went

[17]Jane McCallum frequently referred to people by the first letter of their name, with or without a period. Arthur, Sr., is "Mr. M" or "Dad." These initials can usually be interpreted from the immediate context. Bracketed insertions lighten the reader's task.
[18]That Saturday was Oct. 14.
[19]In its first game of the season, the Austin High School team tied Giddings, 7-7. The *Austin American* reported that Austin's touchdown resulted from "McCallum's line plunges" and "Pete Smith's end runs" (*Austin American,* Oct. 16, 1916, p. 6).
[20]Margaret R. Holliday, M.S., M.D., was physician for women at the University of Texas and also maintained a private practice. She had joined the Austin Woman Suffrage Association at the same time as Jane McCallum and served as a vice president (*Austin City Directory: 1916* [Houston, 1916], 257; Meeting of Oct. 20, 1914, AWSA Minute Book, 1908-

shopping. Due at the University's recep[tion] to Dr & Mrs Vinson[21] this evening as well as city teacher's recep[tion] at Cactus Tea Room—by invitation of Miss M.[innie] Dill. Interesting conversation with Clio Brogan (nee Rice) anent Mrs Clarence Miller['s] activities and withdrawal from Alpha Delt. Alumnae[22]

Arthur making spending money at Moore & Morrisons Saturdays (75¢)[23]

Alas for visions of roast duck! Two of Browns were *water hens*, and a third belonged to Jack!

Monday aft.[ernoon] [Oct. 16?]

The teacher's party was quite nice. Katherine Wright's violin selections [were a] most enjoyable feature.

Alvaro's Sunday school teacher, Miss Minnie Dill, expressed herself as being quite proud of his foot-ball performance.

Roy Snider testified to Brown's mixture of sweetness and badness. Several, according to a habit people seem to have acquired, assured me that I look not a day older than Kathleen. She, by the way, went to the "german."[24] After all the fun, frolic, and frivolity of last year, she is bravely trying to settle down. If the boys would just let her alone!

We went by the recep[tion] to Vinsons at the University Club rooms. Every body was agog over Governor *Ferguson's* outrageous behavior. *We suffragists concluded that, had we the vote, we'd impeach* him—or rather force the legislature to do so. The latest report is that in addition to the resignations of doctors Ellis, Potts, Battle, Mather, Cofer, and

1914). McCallum refers to consulting Dr. Holliday in later entries dated "Friday" and "October 30, 1916."

[21]Dr. Robert E. Vinson resigned from the presidency of Austin Presbyterian Theological Seminary to become president of the University of Texas in 1916, replacing William J. Battle. Vinson remained in that office, despite the objections of Governor James Ferguson, until his resignation in 1923 (*Handbook of Texas*, 2:845).

[22]Jane Y. McCallum had been named to Alpha Delta Pi while enrolled at the University of Texas. As such, she was the first married student to join a university sorority (Nieuwenhuizen, "Minnie Fisher Cunningham and Jane Y. McCallum," 22). Anita M. Miller, the widow of Clarence H. Miller, was active in the same sorority before she earned her B.A. degree in 1911. She is also mentioned in the entry dated "Friday" (below) and, with her daughter Virginia, is named in the entries for Oct. 30, 1916, and July 1917. Presumably, Mrs. Miller was offended by the sorority's invitation to a student she did not approve of (*Directory of the City of Austin: 1918* [Houston, 1918], 325, 327; *General Register of the Students and Former Students of the University of Texas: 1917* [n.p., n.d.], 51).

[23]Moore & Morrison Grocers was located at 1808-1810 Lavaca (*1916 Austin City Directory*, 324).

[24]A "german" was a formal dance. Some were arranged by the University German Club.

Lomax he has demanded that Dr. Vinson resign as president.[25] It takes just such an ignorant, common personage to let an illy gained honor turn his head. He seems to fancy himself a Kaiser. The Vinsons show the strain; Dr. Battle is game—I liked him even better than before; Mrs Cofer is assuring her friends that it will *entail no financi[a]l trouble on them*; Dr. Ellis talks & talks, Mrs Ellis[26] (I care a great deal for her) takes it philosophically & quietly, tho plainly worried. Dr Potts and Ada (just married) seem happy and content as tho governor and politics had never been heard of. [I] Didn't see the other parties concerned; it will go hardest with the Mathers.

Went to church Sunday to hear Dr. Anderson who has taken Dr Vinson's place as head of Seminary.[27] Had chat with Mae while waiting for session to get through with its deliberations. In afternoon two of the foot-ball boys, Dewy Bradford and Pete Smith[,] brought last year's captain and *star* out. Poor "Trap" (Henderson) fell by the way side in his *literary* activities, hence was put off the team last year. He has entered school again, and now they are begging for him to be let back on the team.

It was the greatest fun to hear the boys describe their shower baths (out of *"tin cup[,]"* the hose etc.) and sleeping apartments (parlor floors[,] benches etc.[)] at Giddings.

Later in afternoon Mrs. Gracy and David[28] took Kathleen and me driving. For the third time when D. has had K. out, there was tire trouble—but it was considerate enough to "blow out" while we were within view of the hills, so we enjoyed ourselves & the view while David *toiled*.

[25]Governor Ferguson appeared at the October 1916 meeting of the University of Texas Board of Regents and insisted, as he had in the spring of 1916, that several faculty members had to go. On this occasion he made a variety of accusations against the individuals, ranging from political disloyalty to financial mismanagement. (Frantz, *Forty-Acre Follies*, 73-74; Gould, *Progressives and Prohibitionists*, 192-94). A. Caswell Ellis, an equal suffrage ally, was professor of the philosophy of education. C. S. Potts and R. E. Cofer were on the law school faculty. William J.Battle had returned to the classics department after his term as acting president of the university. W. T. Mather was a member of the physics department. Folklorist John A. Lomax was secretary to the faculty (*Austin American*, July 14, 1917, p. 1; *Handbook of Texas*, 3:64, 750-51).

[26]Like her husband Alexander Caswell Ellis, Mary Heard Ellis was active in the Austin Equal Suffrage Association. About the time this was written she taught history at Austin High School (*Austin American Statesman*, Apr. 6, 1958, pp. C-1, C-12).

[27]The Reverend Neal Larkin Anderson, a North Carolinian, was president of the Austin Theological Seminary for only one year beginning in May 1916 (Thomas White Currie, Jr., *Austin Presbyterian Theological Seminary: A Seventy-fifth Anniversary History* [San Antonio, 1978], 48).

[28]Emma C. (Mrs. David B.) Gracy's son David C. was a student at the University of Texas (*1916 Austin City Directory*, 231).

Friday [Oct. 20?]

I'm tired, and I don't want to be. The day is simply gorgeous and there are a dozen things—*each more interesting than the other* that I want to be doing. But I felt so fine that I decided to wash Alvaro's foot ball sweater, socks etc. (guess now I'll have to *boil* the bath tub). Then I—with Mamma's & Ida's assistance—moved a bed in off the gallery to be ready for Mr. M. when he feels a touch of asthma, and by the time I finished sweeping and oiling floors—*I'm all in.* But Dr. Holliday is fast getting me strong again.

The past week has been to[o] full to *put down.* Have been to doctor twice; done quite a bit of sewing; and had a meeting of executive board ([Austin] Woman Suffrage Ass[ociation]). 1916 We appointed chairman of committees etc. Since Mrs. Pennybacker[29] told me at the Keasby-Allerdice Wedding that she was ready—now, that her term of president of Nat.[ional] Fed[eration of Women's] Clubs is over—to work with us I hoped she would accept a chairmanship, and sent her a night letter to the effect that she was to wire her choice in case she would (she is in Iowa for short time). But have had no reply, so suppose she can't.

Poor Mrs. Miller! I fear she has estranged about a dozen friends the past two weeks. Because the girls passed a girl (Dibrell from Seguin)[30] to whom she was violently opposed, she has been on a tear equaled only by the one she went on when Kathleen went Theta. (She is still harping on the Theta's—Susan Gilfillan affording the latest excuse).

Austin High plays San Antonio High this afternoon, and I'm cutting High School Mother's Club and first meeting of Shakspere Club[31] (social with Mrs. H. Y. Benedict) to go. Alvaro—bless his heart—says he isn't *sure* he can play as well if I am there, and yet he wants me to be. I've

[29]Anna J. (Mrs. Percy V.) Pennybacker had distinguished herself by her activities in the Chautauqua Institution, as well as by her presidency of the National Federation of Women's Clubs from 1912 to 1916. In March 1917 she was named a director of the Leslie Woman Suffrage Commission in New York City. She maintained a residence in Austin between 1900 and her death in 1938, although work and travel often required her absence from the city (*Handbook of Texas*, 2:360; Carrie Chapman Catt to Anna Pennybacker, Mar. 31, 1917, papers concerning woman suffrage, Mrs. Percy V. (Anna J.) Pennybacker Papers, BTHC). One suffragist felt that Pennybacker "did all she could to hurt the movement in Texas" by not bringing it before the 1912 convention of the National Federation of Women's Clubs and her attitude that "I'm a suffragist *but* there are *other things more important.*" (Elizabeth Herndon Potter to Minnie Fisher Cunningham, [Summer 1916?], Box 15, McCP, II; Rebecca Richmond, *A Woman of Texas: Mrs. Percy V. Pennybacker* [San Antonio, 1941], 133-34, 221; Potter to Cunningham, Mar. 19, 1916, Box 15, McCP, II).

[30]This young woman was doubtless the daughter of Judge J. S. and Ella Dibrell. (See Part 1, *n*19 and Part 2, *n*50.)

[31]The club spelled its name this way (Austin Shakspere Club, *1906-07 Yearbook*, folder on Shakspere Club, Box 8, McCP, II).

promised if he gets "knocked out" to shut my eyes, hold tight to the seat; tumble under *grand stand;* or do *anything* rather than *appear disturbed.* Says he'd *never play another game* if I'd go to him on the field. Most of the other players have from one to three years experience the advantage of him, so [I] dont know what to expect. The boys are all up in the air because "Swede" Johnson can't play on account of not making his courses. They've lost three of their best this way. K.[athleen] made B- on her first education quiz and B+ on first Eng.[lish] theme. She was supposed to have cut out Majestic[32] but when Pendleton Howard—last years editor of Cactus[33]—asked the pleasure, she took another thought & accepted— wonder what the boys she refused [bottom of page torn]

October 30, 1916
Monday.

I was *so* hopeful that I'd be able to jot down a *little bit* in this every day, but *so many calls!*

~~The day after I wrote last, I again got Alvaro's togs in order but spent a lot of [the] morning 'phoning on suffrage affairs. Hubert Jones (yell leader at University and whose grandmother was a McCallum) 'phoned right after lunch to know if he might come and talk some of his problems over with me. While he was here I got so cold—even with coat suit on that I turned blue [bottom of page torn] I walked *fast* nearly to where Mr. M. was to meet us to go to the game~~

Well, the joke's on me. I've had dengue fever, and didn't know it until the rash broke out on me while in Dr. Holliday's office.[34] I never felt a much greater relief than when I found out the cause of my terrble backache and general bad feelings. I evidently took it—with a chill—the Friday after my last entry. Hubert was out to talk over some of his problems and I got so cold he took off his sweater to put around me after I'd utilized the boys' coats in coat closet. Alvaro arrived and said I looked awful & should stay at home. But no sir ree! I got A.[lvaro] off and Arthur fixed up and talked over with Brown a proposed camping trip he & 3 friends—James Rice, Wroe Alexander, and Jack Straus, were planning. Then H.[ubert] suggested we walk to where Mr. M was to meet me to go to the game[.] We almost *ran* and I got warm, but my family seemed

[32]The Majestic Theatre presented a variety of entertainment and was later renamed the Paramount.
[33]*The Cactus* is the University of Texas yearbook.
[34]Dengue fever is a viral disease spread by mosquitoes and characterized by the symptoms McCallum describes (Morris Fishbein, *Dr. Fishbein's Popular Illustrated Medical Encyclopedia* [New York, 1979], 217).

worried over my appearance and were also pleased to find out a week later what the trouble was.

The game. I didn't know *how* I'd feel, but queer as it may seem, I never once felt the slightest uneasiness—not even when Bess Hutchings—sitting next me—declared excitedly that some one was hurt[,] then said to me "Oh, I believe it's Alvaro!" Foolish girl. I'm glad, I'm like that always when there is danger, tho Dr. Holliday says its what has caused my trouble. I "keep too much on inside—too self controlled" *The Texan*[35] mentioned only Pete and Alvaro's "stellar work."

I have not time to record last week's performances. Sallie—and I can't remember who else—was here Sunday—oh yes—Mary Lee[36] had dinner with us, and spent the night. The girls had to study as K.[athleen] had been to dance the night before and *Anglers*[37] had theirs on for Monday.

Hubert [Jones] came out either Monday or Tuesday, and it would take a lot more pages than I have time to write to tell of Mrs. Miller's diabolical cleverness in trying to make him appear friend to Virginia instead of the Brydson child. Even I (villain?) could not conceive of her deep laid scheme until Dr. Holliday put me on to it.

A.[ustin] H.[igh] S.[chool] played San Marcos High Friday and the latter didn't do a thing but have five of Coronel's[38] best players register two days before in [San Marcos] High so they could beat us. Our boys despite this, came out ahead in a six to nothing average. But such things are *bad* for them.

I'd love to have time to write all about Baylor University versus Texas game. Jesse[39] came with them—to mammas delight. Foot-ball seems to be this family's stumbling block in the way to financial progress. We attended the game, *from and including* Mr. M. and Baby Henry! Oh, it was awful! Ten to three in favor of Baylor. In the excitement of getting quick lime off Henry and getting him ready, seeing that a boy (Brown) got K[athleen]'s new coat suit out, phoning to see if we could get seats at that late hour, finishing trimming my hat (which is O.K. if I *did* do it)[,]

[35]The newspaper published by University of Texas students at the time was called *The Texan.*

[36]Mary Lee Read, a sorority sister of Kathleen's in Kappa Alpha Theta, was a frequent guest of the McCallums. Her name is often abbreviated as M.L. or M.L.R. She later married Hubert Jones (*General Register of Students*, 244).

[37]According to the 1917 *Cactus*, Kathleen McCallum was a member of The Anglers, a University of Texas women's social organization (n.p., n.d., 294).

[38]Coronal Institute, a private school in San Marcos, was discontinued in 1917 (*Handbook of Texas*, 1:414-15).

[39]The Reverend Jesse Yelvington, Jane McCallum's brother, held a variety of Baptist ministries in Texas parishes over the years.

laughing at Hubert (who had come to meet Jess) and Jess talking about night shirt parade[,] dressing myself[,] three o'clock (when Jess had to join Baylor rooters) almost arrived before I knew it, so I rushed off without giving Ida orders for supper. Well—Mr. M. & I stopped to get some *canned* supper, and Jess beat us, and when he and I, Kathleen & Tulane Smith arrived, Jess had put Baylor banner up over door and turned light full on it. They pulled it down while I proceeded to chastise him with the cane carrying my big Varsity pennant. He made me do the *Bear Trail* and I guess the Smith boy was some what shocked when he rushed me almost over him & then picked me up and ran around the yard with me. It was worth a lot to see the kid so happy. His ears most caved in sure enough this time.

Henrietta Lightfoot had dinner with K.[athleen] yesterday. Charlie (Freshman) Faust had a sister from Baylor in town and brought her out to see K. and me.

Nov. 1, 1916

October days still. Our anniversary ([October] 29) was, as usual, a beautiful day.

Our house was the dwelling place of ghosts and hobgoblins last (Halloween) night. Henry decided he wanted a party, so invited between fifteen & 20 children of Gypsy Grove, Aldridge Place and Penn Place to come in costume. The furnace room back of the cellar was an ideal place for the witch (Mary Lee Read) to do her branding. I was the witch to escort them into cellar one at a time, and Arthur the one to give them the *wet sand* hand shake. If getting frightened, then begging to be frightened again constitutes a good time they certainly had it. They bobbed for apples, and had witche's brew & cakes for refreshments. K.[athleen] went to A.[lpha] T.[au] O.[mega] dance; boys "played out." (play-out night)

Aunt Nonie[40] & uncle John came in afternoon unexpectedly[,] so as Leila was away[,] they spent aft.[ernoon] with us.

This morning first, I taught Henry his lessons that were neglect[ed] last night; read over Mary Lees Eng.[lish] theme and made suggestions; saw that Henry's "corners" were in condition; mended tear in Arthur's stocking; covered some freshly transplanted lettuce; watered ferns; cleaned upstairs—while talking to Mrs. D. C. McCaleb[41] who was over talking of her mother-in-law troubles; made engagement to have confer-

---

[40]Aunt Nonie was Alvaro Yelvington's sister.
[41]The McCalebs were neighbors of the McCallums at 503 West 32nd Street (*1916 Austin City Directory*, 300).

ence with Mrs. Pennybacker at 3.30 this P.M.; got some more commit-
teemen; gave corresponding Sec[retary of the Austin Equal Suffrage
Association] (Mrs. Speer) directions for a letter to be answered; got *light*
lunch for mamma, K. and me; and answered 'phone about eight times.
Glad I decided to write this down for was feeling that I had not done a
thing.

Nov. 2, 1916
    Well, I don't see any way out except to take public speaking! It is now
12.30 and I've been since 9 o'clock getting some one to accept invitation
of Miss Pyle (Y.W.C.A. Sec[retary]) to speak on suffrage before a club she
has organized. It is certainly exasperating, especially when I had *so* much
to do.
    Certainly feel encouraged over result of visits to Mrs. Pennybacker
yesterday. Had to go back for a second visit, and we talked long &
earnestly, but at the close she had promised to make several speeches in
the district[,] one here during session of Legislature, and to accept
chairman of committee (to be created) on *Outlook*. She is going to
communicate with Mrs. Catt[42] about comeing here also. I *do* feel happy
over it; and tho I get provoked over spending an entire half day as this
morning, yet think I made a number of friends—or rather renewed the
interest of lukewarm friends—to the cause. Mrs. Tru*man* Kelly lived in
Cal. when the cause was won, and says her conscience has always hurt
her because she took no active part in helping to win it. I told her we'd
furnish opportunity for her to make rectification

Friday Feb 2, 1917
    The days, weeks, and months have simply flown. But they are so
"brim full" of experiences that I must hurriedly make note of some of
them.
    This morning after arranging for the day's meals, and getting my
family in order, I went to City Hall (Mrs. Holden's office) to meet committee on budgeting United Charities[43] expenditures for coming years.

[42]Carrie Chapman Catt succeeded Susan B. Anthony as president of the National
American Woman Suffrage Association in 1900, having worked her way up in the ranks
through the Iowa chapter. Because of her own poor health, as well as her husband's and
mother's, she resigned in 1904. When she returned to the suffrage cause, it was to work in
the international association. After helping in the New York suffrage referendum in 1915,
she was again elected president of NAWSA, a job which she held until the group
disbanded in 1920. Catt was noted for her skills as an organizer and energizer (Robert
Booth Fowler, *Carrie Catt: Feminist Politician* [Boston, 1986], 19-31).
    [43]The United Charities office was at City Hall perhaps because Mayor A. P. Wooldridge

Ralph Goeth and Mr. Morse were the others present. There's going to be some fun when they (board) realize we plan for larger salaries.

Went from there to meet *rose day*[44] chairman, Mrs. Daniels. We went to Capitol to see State Purchasing agent (Geo. Leavy) about State orders. Arranged satisfactorily—saw Capitol Grounds man, and he also, will give us order. Then went to gallery of House of R.[epresentatives] and heard the oratorical efforts of those fighting for and against prohibition; then home; then out to Insane Asylum to tell Mrs. Preston[45] [that] Mr. Leavy said to make out orders for shrubbery for his OK. Tooke her price list. Then by for Mrs. Speer (Mrs Wilson took me in her car), then for Mrs. Daniels, and together we took list and Mr. Leavys message to Deaf & Dumb Institute in South Austin, Mr. Erbantke(?) Supt.[46] He is going to make us out an order. Coming back we couldn't resist going by a Gypsy Camp. Then I let them go on to Blind Institute while I caught [street] car for Shakspere Club meeting

Monday,
Mch 12, 1917

A prediction: there were several boys—young men I should say—out here yesterday afternoon who will be heard from in no uncertain way in the years to come. They were: G[e]orge Peddy, U.T. student and [state] representative;[47] Roy Snider, last year graduate, now teaching in High School, and Hubert Jones—four years yell leader, and recently elected varsity circus[48] manager for *next* year. Of course Charlie (Freeman, Phi

was once its president (*1912-13 Austin City Directory*, 303). See the diary entry for July 7, 1917, for his marriage to Mrs. Nellie Holden, general secretary of the United Charities.
[44] Roses were sold on Feb. 8, 1917, to raise funds for the Austin Equal Suffrage Association (*Austin American*, Feb. 8, 1917, p. 4).
[45] Annie Preston's husband John was superintendent of the Texas State Lunatic Asylum (*1918 Austin City Directory*, 359). The mother of seven, Annie Preston was active in school parent groups and was elected district president of the Texas Congress of Mothers in May 1916 (Sinclair Moreland, *Texas Women's Hall of Fame* [Austin, 1917], 72-74). See also the diary entries for May 11, 1917, and July 20, 1918.
[46] Gus F. Urbantke was superintendent of the Texas School for the Deaf (*1918 Austin City Directory*, 425).
[47] McCallum's prediction proved true for George Peddy. Peddy resigned his seat as Shelby County's representative to accept an army commission. After World War I, he obtained his law degree and served as assistant U.S. attorney. Peddy's anti-Ku Klux Klan stance pitted him in a losing battle against Earle Mayfield for the Democratic nomination for the U.S. Senate in 1922. In 1925 he became a partner in the Houston firm of Vinson, Elkins, Weems, and Francis. Peddy ran again for the U.S. Senate in 1948, winning enough votes to force opponents Lyndon Johnson and Coke Stevenson into a runoff (*Handbook of Texas*, 3:716-17).
[48] The varsity circus was a biennial event of high spirits and good humor carried out by University of Texas fraternities and sororities. An afternoon parade featured a queen,

Gam of Dallas & Kathleen's latest) appeared on the scene also. But where to begin? I've not even mentioned that Mrs. Minnie Fisher *Cunningham*[,] Stat[e] president[,][49] moved [Texas Equal Suffrage Association] *Head-quarters here for session of legislature—that we started* things off by giving a *luncheon* at [the] Driskill said by dozens to be cleverest ever held here—that they kindly gave me most credit as the idea of impersonating legislature and program was wholly mine. As president, I had to play Mr. Speaker; Mr. *Charlie Norton*[,] City editor of [Austin] American[,] was my clerk and read caption of Suffrage bill which was discust really brilliantly (making toast program) by Mesdames *Pennybacker, J. A. Jackson, M. F. Cunningham*, Miss *Lutie Sterns* of Wisconsin; Messrs Hamlet[t] and Dudl[e]y Woodward. Mrs. Sander sang a clever little Suffrage song. There were two hundred & fifty present, including Mrs. Thomas M. Campbell wife of ex gov. from Palestine, Mrs J. B. Dibrell, Seguin; Mrs G. R. Scott Corpus [Christi]; Miss Fenwick San Antonio etc. etc. etc.[50]

But can't tell all these things—Mrs. Cunningham decided that Mrs. Elizabeth Speer and I make best lobbyists; so has put us through.[51] A

floats, and suitable music. An evening presentation combined humorous skits with rodeo performances (*The Cactus* [Austin, 1916], 240-41).

[49]Jane McCallum's friendship with Minnie Fisher Cunningham probably began about 1915, when McCallum was president of the local suffrage group and Cunningham president of the state association. It continued with much affection and mutual respect for many years. Cunningham's tenure with the Texas Equal Suffrage Association lasted from 1911 to 1919, although she spent some of this period in Washington, D.C., on behalf of the national effort. Minnie Fisher Cunningham was a candidate for the U.S. Senate in 1928 and for governor of Texas in 1944 (*Handbook of Texas*, 3:216).

[50]The luncheon was held on January 12. In addition to her suffrage work, Pearl Jackson was a writer, a member of the Kwill Klub, and a past president of the Texas Woman's Press Association. Lutie Sterns's visit to Austin was as a paid lecturer from the National American Woman Suffrage Association. Rev. William A. Hamlett was pastor of the First Baptist Church. Woodward was an Austin lawyer and civic leader who also played a crucial role in bringing the university's case against Governor James Ferguson to the state legislature. Thomas M. Campbell had been governor of Texas from 1907 to 1911 and had failed as a U.S. Senate candidate in 1916. Ella Dibrell was a former Austinite and friend of McCallum's from Seguin days. Her husband had a law practice in Seguin in 1917. A noted journalist, Marin Fenwick was also active in the Texas Equal Suffrage Association (*The Standard Blue Book—Texas, Edition 1920* [San Antonio, 1920], 198; *Austin Statesman*, Jan. 13, 1917, p. 8; *Austin American*, Jan. 13, 1917, p. 3; *1918 Austin City Directory*, 249; Franz, *Forty-Acre Follies*, 75; *Handbook of Texas*, 1:286-87, 500).

[51]The Texas Equal Suffrage Association was lobbying the regular session of the Texas legislature for passage of the primary suffrage bill, which would permit women to vote in primary elections. It was reported out of committee in the Senate on January 31 but never came up for a vote. On the House side, a state constitutional amendment for primary suffrage (which would then be submitted to the voters) failed to garner the necessary two-thirds majority when it came to a vote on February 6 (JYM, "Activities of Women in Texas Politics," in Frank Carter Adams, ed., *Texas Democracy: A Centennial History of Politics and Personalities of the Democratic Party: 1836-1936* [Austin, 1937], 473-74).

book could be written on our experiences. (*Must some day* write of the only man we've encountered who is in total ignorance of the meaning of the term *gentleman*) To get down to date, when our bill came up, some *wonderful* speeches were made—we had not dreamed there were so many talented men in the house. *Fifteen* were ready to speak for us and Bagby, Beard of Houston, Barry Miller, George Mendell, and poor little "Ballots backed by bullets" Dunham spoke against us.[52] Of course their very names bring visions of *ballots backed by breweries* instead of bullets. They call Bagby the "Lion of Lavaca" but that day with his snapping & snarling, and insults to Miss Sterns he was like the diseased, disgruntled old lion that had crawled off to die. Oh, they were the hunt, but I've never known a more soul satisfying period than when our advocates, straight[,] clean, fearless, proceeded to wipe up the earth with their *sham* chivalry, sob stuff and positive misrepresentation. Thomason of El Paso; Laney of Dallas were great,[53] but George Peddy—of whom I spoke at the beginning of this entry.—was *simply superb*. He has been the sensation of the legislature. Every one predicts a great future for him, and as Mr. McCallum said after talking to him yesterday—"He couldn't be dishonest if he tried." But those men *hired*, bought & paid for themselves, will try in the most subtle way to ruin him, and thereby hangs the tale of his being asked out here yesterday. Mrs. Speer came also & brought two attractive girls: Frances Clark, and Frances Busse(?).[54] But I wont tell our counter scheme yet.

Saturday at 4.30 P M sixteen of us took Mrs. Cunningham up the lake— on the *Monarch*—and had a *wonderful* time.[55] Not one thing occurred to spoil the pleasure of the occasion.

Tomorrow Mrs. C.[unningham] *speaks before the Rotary Club, and the president, Mr. D.* Woodward asked me to come, also, as his guest. We are

---

[52]Will T. Bagby (from Hallettsville in Lavaca County), Stanley Beard (Houston), Barry Miller (Dallas), George Mendell (Austin), and W. V. Dunnam (Coryell County) were members of the Texas House of Representatives (*Members of the Texas Legislature, 1846-1980* [n.p., n.d.], 256, 257, 258). The issues of suffrage and prohibition (with opponents of the two measures cast as pro-German and anti-American) were entwined in the deliberations of the state legislature as well as in the politics of the executive branch.

[53]Robert Ewing Thomason (El Paso), and C. O. Laney (Dallas) were also state representatives (*Members of the Texas Legislature*, 258, 260). As Speaker of the House in 1919, Thomason became an even more important ally of the suffragists. See diary entries for Mar. 25-26 and June 24, 1919, and Part 3, *n*137.

[54]Frances Bussey was a student at the University of Texas (*1918 Austin City Directory*, 175).

[55]The Lake Austin Transportation Company, located at Austin Dam (rebuilt as Tom Miller Dam), provided excursion boats for outings on the lake (*1918 Austin City Directory*, 461).

both invited to attend *Lion's* Club where she *will speak* at luncheon Wednesday.[56]

Several Saturdays past after being urged both by letter and long distance telephone, I gathered together at Driskill for lunch Misses Emma Burleson, Julia Pease[,] Mrs. Thompson & self & Mrs. J. C. Griswold came over from San Antonio to organize a Pan-American round table. Mrs. Walter Wilcox & Mrs. Pierre Bremond couldn't come but *promised to join*[57]—(Miss Julia & Miss Emma could not [take the lead in organizing it], neither could I) but when Mrs. Griswold—at our suggestion—went to see Mrs. Wilcox to take lead Nothing doing

Up to this point in her diary, Jane McCallum has made no mention of the war which had been ravaging Europe for more than two years. One wonders if she had any inkling that within a month the United States would enter World War I. Perhaps she was still able, unlike many Americans, to maintain a firm neutral attitude toward the conflict.

The United States' neutrality in the affairs of Europe had eroded considerably since the outbreak of World War I in 1914. The British blockade, designed to hinder the neutrals' trade with Germany, had generated anger, but the growth of American trade with the Allies had given a much needed boost to the economy. German submarine attacks on passenger ships and merchant vessels ultimately tipped the balance of American sentiment unmistakably in the Allies' favor by early 1917. The March publication of the Zimmerman telegram, which threatened a Mexican-German alliance, heightened the demand for battle.[58] On April 7, 1917, the Congress declared war on Germany in response to President Wilson's call.

[56]Newspaper reports indicate that Lavinia Engle of the National American Woman Suffrage Association spoke to the Rotary Club on Tuesday, March 13. Jane McCallum accompanied her to the meeting. On Wednesday, March 14, both McCallum and Minnie Fisher Cunningham addressed the Lions (*Austin American*, Mar. 14, 1917, p. 5; *Austin Statesman*, Mar. 14, 1917, p. 10).

[57]Emma Burleson was the sister of Woodrow Wilson's Postmaster General, A. S. Burleson, of Austin (AF-Biography, Albert Sidney Burleson (7), Austin History Center, Austin Public Library [hereafter cited as AHC, APL]). Julia Pease was the daughter of former Governor Elisha Pease. Dorothy Wilcox was the wife of a Congress Avenue men's clothier, while Nina Bremond's husband was vice president of The State National Bank (*1918 Austin City Directory*, 166, 349, 440).

[58]William E. Leuchtenburg, *The Perils of Prosperity: 1914-32* (Chicago, 1958), 12-34; Walter La Feber and Richard Polenberg, *The American Century: A History of the United States Since the 1890s* (New York, 1975), 86-92.

The country was ill-prepared to go to war. Despite earlier legislation to beef up troop strength and spur arms manufacturing, the army and navy were woefully short-handed and ill-equipped. Not only were several million recruits needed in a hurry, but they required training, weapons, clothing, and food. And these necessities had to be paid for.[59]

For average citizens like Jane McCallum, America's entry into the war meant abrupt changes in day-to-day life. Within weeks of the declaration of war, Americans began to knit for the boys "over there" and learned to can fruits and vegetables grown in their own gardens. McCallum helped organize a patriotic parade and entertained aviation trainees in her home. She sacrificed eating wheat products and devoted time to selling Liberty Bonds instead of to suffrage issues.

For McCallum, as for many, the heaviest burden of wartime was the sight of so many young men leaving to fight for their country. Whether they enlisted or were drafted, she dreaded the changes the war would make in their lives.

[The numbered pages 39 through 44, which included at least some manuscript material, have been torn out. McCallum instructs the reader to start on page 45, then skip back to page 38. She relates an incident pertaining to a recently enlisted friend that occurred on a hike to Mt. Bonnell. Presumably, she began her narration of the hike in the deleted pages, since in the passage below, she is "going back" to the subject.[60]]

[p. 45]
[April 1917?]
* * Read before 38
With a vacant lot stare a fellow can make folks believe that he is actually entertaining a thought.—Going back to the Mt. Bonnell hike, as we were returning, the big whistle blew—a long wailing call to mobilization and tho only one of the boys of our crowd Charles Barrow, was summonsed by it, my heart suddenly seemed (turn back to p. 38)
[p. 38] turned to lead. I was glad it was dark so no one could see my face.

[59]Arthur S. Link, *American Epoch: A History of the United States Since the 1890's* (New York, 1955), 185-88.
[60]On page 38 McCallum wrote "Read page 45 first." Page 45 begins with a sentence fragment, and two-thirds of the way down the page the start of the next passage is marked by McCallum's note to "Read before 38." The pages which have been torn out must contain both the beginning of the fragment which is concluded at the top of page 45 and some reference to the Mt. Bonnell hike.

Of course we do not take it the least bit seriously,—apparently—but as I looked at those fine young fellows—and thought of my own coming on—well I had to laugh and talk much as I could. We went by home, and Charles eyes were fairly dancing with delighted excitement. But I learned something of the part a mother should *not* play. He finally got his sister over the telephone; his expression changed and we learned that his mother was almost prostrated with grief, and that when he went to the Border she had cried for three consecutive days and nights.

[A sentence fragment leads off page 45.]
the rows seem shorter

* * *

If I were not tall enough to look squarely into a man's eyes I don't think I'd gain the advantage by wearing high heel shoes.

* * *

If I had a million dollars I'd get me thirteen pairs of real silk hose, and two dozen real linen handkerchiefs

* * *

Some people get more pleasure out of a little pain than others do out of an automobile

Friday, May 11,
1917
I have just finished reading a diary in which the writer—who was, at the time, leading an apparently monotonous life—recorded thoughts rather than deeds, (or, rather, simply occurences). How vastly more interesting than this snatching here and there of events and recording them—not even taking time—or *having* time—to estimate them—or select the more important—*and never* a way-deep-down-in-your-heart peep.

I am inexpressably sad, and glad, by turns. It's the *war*. Would to God the thing those three little letters stand for had never been heard of! But— yet—we can even now see that it was the only way.

A little over a week ago—I *believe*—dates *never* stay with me—I heard a familiar "Hello Sis!," and I knew that it was *Henry*,[61] and that the *war* had something to do with it. He had come to see Gen. Hutchings before

---

[61] Jane McCallum's other brother, Henry Yelvington, was a journalist and special enforcement officer with the state liquor control board (Clipping, *San Marcos Record*, Mar. 3, 1944, folder on Henry Yelvington, McCP, II).

enlisting for Leon Springs Officer's Training Camp.[62] Can't bear the idea of not going! Charles Freeman had signed up—Hubert [Jones] had—but I'll not name them—the flower of the University has gone. Charles got his brother to bring over his car from Dallas so he and K[athleen] could have some "last rides together." *They did!* The day after Henry came, Chas was to have lunch with us (he also did *that* day), and it was too funny about the squabs (*writing of squabs*, and thinking of,—grieving *over the tragedies that follow* in the wake of war—such is life) We got enough for the four of us, then Henry 'phoned out that *Chester Crowell*[63] would be out to lunch with him and we got *another*—then Hubert came to see H.[enry]—and we *couldn't get another*, so he had to go back home for lunch.

All week long it has been "Leon Springs," "Leon Springs." When asked to do things I feel like saying "Well just wait, please, until I get this camp straightened out" One evening Mr. M had Capt Claiborne Duval and Messers Stevens and Quillian(?) school men—rather boys who are going. They had their last meal in Austin, before going, with us. Mr. & Mrs. Joe Harrell[64] were guests at the same time, and we had a lively party.

(Henry has just brought up Charlie's *second* letter.) The night he came to say "good-bye" I broke my rules—oh well—[65]

C[harlie Freeman] reported on 8th—H[ubert] is to report tomorrow but left on early train this morning, so Mary Lee & he had his farewell meal with us last night, and *he* stayed—well Dan telephoned this morning that he sat up for him until fifteen after one, then he—Dan—went to sleep.

Watkins Harris had his last night in town last night also, and came out to see K.[athleen] We told him "good-bye."

Bless their brave young hearts, and bless the dear little girls they are leaving behind. There may not be many exposed to view, but I'll wager

---

[62]Located twenty-six miles north of San Antonio, Leon Springs was a U.S. Army officers training camp. It opened on May 15, 1917 (*Handbook of Texas*, 2:49). Brigadier General Henry Hutchings, who founded the *Austin Evening News* in 1890, organized and commanded the 71st Infantry Brigade during World War I (*Handbook of Texas*, 1:870).

[63]A journalist like Henry Yelvington, Chester Crowell was manager-editor of *Texas Monthly Review* (1918 *Austin City Directory*, 199). McCallum refers to this gathering in her diary entry for Jan. 5, 1919.

[64]In addition to his involvement in the family business, a Congress Avenue men's clothiers, Joe Harrell had been elected president of the Austin School Board for the following fall (*Austin American*, Apr. 10, 1917, p. 8).

[65]The incident on Mt. Bonnell (diary page 45) provides a clue that Jane McCallum did not want these "fine young fellows" to know of her fears for them as they left for war. She apparently could not hold back her tears when saying goodby to Charlie Freeman. Her fondness for him and her strong identification as a mother made her cheerful exterior hard to maintain.

that for nearly every student at Leon Springs, there is being worn, on some girls *camisole*, a fraternity pin!

I wish I knew a little bit about myself. They wanted me to protest against sending our boys to France and I *would not*—I fought the resolution, and helped down it.[66] Now, Mrs. Graves, Mrs Doom[,] Mrs. Preston and others, want to protest against prisoners being sent here. They want me to take the lead. I *will not*. I think it would be cowardly. I laugh at their fears and pessimism, and play the cheerful part so well that Mrs. Graves rebuked me for being so *light hearted*! And when no one saw, or *could know* I went to my room and nearly cried myself sick.

A record should have gone in before this. The day of the final tryouts for the State track meet Mrs. Harris Roger[']s mother[67] and I slipped down to Clark Field and saw our boys win easily, the relay race that they took state championship in next day. Everybody commented on how big and handsome Alvaro looked. Even George Peddy (who was "playing off" from Legislature) and Mr. Whittaker who came and sat by us. They are both at Leon Springs now.

Alvaro has neglected his studies tho, and I am *so* worried about it. I don't know that he will graduate. *Have I failed him?* I feel some times that I've failed every body, and every thing. *Why* do we have to *live a life nearly through* before we *know how*? And then—*do we know*? Think I'd better stop and go look at my poppies.

(Message to president Wilson about Frederick Howe signatures)

Later—Orders came from Mrs Catt[,] Nat.[ional] [American Woman] Suf.[frage] Pres.[ident] to get signatures urging the President to place Howe on Russian commission with Root.[68] Miss Lillie Robertson[69] and I got the following signatures to a night letter

---

[66] President Wilson had decided only in the first days of May to send American troops to France at the earliest possible time, rather than to wait until they had been thoroughly trained (*Austin American*, May 3, 1917, p. 1).

[67] "Rogers mother" was inserted interlinearly at a later date.

[68] In 1914 Woodrow Wilson had appointed his former Johns Hopkins student, now lawyer, Frederic C. Howe, to the position of commissioner of immigration of the Port of New York. He was a progressive and sympathetic to the woman suffrage cause. Diplomat Elihu Root was an American spokesperson in Russia in the spring of 1917. After the abdication of Tsar Nicholas in March, Wilson perhaps wished to have a personal representative on the scene to observe events and assure Russia's continued participation in the war. The women naturally preferred their ally for this influential post. Ferguson was apparently ignorant of Howe's politics (Arthur S. Link, *Wilson: The Road to the White House* [Princeton, 1947], 24; Robert Livingston Schuyler and Edward T. James, eds., *Dictionary of American Biography, Supplement 2 to December 31, 1940* [New York, 1958], 326-27, 581; *Austin American*, June 17, 1917, pp. 1, 2).

[69] Lillie Robertson's father, Dr. Joseph Robertson, had purchased the French Legation in

A. P. Wooldridge, Mayor
A. N. McCallum Supt Schools
H. A. Wroe, Pres Chamber Commerce
Mrs. P. V. Pennybacker Past Pres. National Fed. Women's Clubs
W. P. Hobby, Lieutenant Gov.
Fuller, Speaker House of R.
James E. Ferguson, Governor of Texas.

We nearly died laughing when the Governor signed. We certainly would have answered any questions and as he is so violently opposed to suffrage never expected him to sign. But we sent petition (or night letter) in by Mr. Davis.[70] Mr. D. came back and said Gov. didn't know Howe, and wished to know. Just in a spirit of meanness I said, "Tell the governor he will be *ashamed* of having said that—why Howe is one of the greatest living Americans. Read the message through"— The message referred to Howe as "your [Wilson's] emmigration inspector."

Well—Mr. Davis re-appeared in about two minutes with the signature!

May 1917

Last Sat. morning I got breakfast ([I] do all my cooking now) worked with flowers, sewed a little, fed chickens, cooked dinner—went to D.[ivision of] E.[xtension] department to get instructions about our trip to country to arouse "canning interests;"[71] from there to K. Hall to canning demonstration; then to Theta tea; then to kitchen shower to Mary Evans and Marguerite Richardson—two frat sisters. It was a charming little affair at Clio (Rice) Brogans. They had so much fun over my rhymes. I gave potato masher to Mary who is to marry Marshall Munro and to distinguish it—as ordered—wrote, As your Mun roes the boat,

with your cargo afloat
May *you* Ma(r)sh all the hard lumps away.

What did I put on the other?
Sunday Charles [Freeman] had dinner with us—6 carloads of boys came over from Camp.

1848 and resided there with his family. After his death in 1870 Lillie Robertson hosted public tours of the building and participated in a variety of patriotic organizations (AF - Biography, Joseph William Robertson, AHC, APL; *Handbook of Texas*, 1:647).

[70]James H. Davis, Jr., was Ferguson's assistant private secretary (*1916 Austin City Directory*, 45).

[71]The Division of Extension was part of the University of Texas. Home canning of homegrown produce was being encouraged along with other measures to conserve food for the armed forces.

Tuesday we had a really *wonderful* Suffrage meeting[.] I can sympathise with Mrs. Scott (Club editor) who said to me, "I want to write that meeting up for Sunday's paper, and I feel so helpless to do it justice; It was *wonderful*." I'll paste in what she says.[72]

Wednesday I prepared evening meal for my family, and went with Mrs John Brady

[At the top of the next page, hand-numbered as 61, Jane McCallum instructs the reader to "(skip to next page)" because the material on this page is out of order.]

at 11.30 to Richland to arouse interest in canning. We went by for Mrs. Doughty.[73] The women [were] all Germans and [had] no gardens [—] dry weather killed them. Very good meeting however.

Today after *going mad* over answering 'phone and phoning[,] our "canning club" met at Wooldridge School. Had lots of fun and experience! Continued story. Mrs. Cunningham and Mrs. Speer out in morning. The work planned is grand. Have to go to another Conference tomorrow with

Friday
    Just from Conference with State Pres[ident] Cunningham & Mrs. Speer. One of the greatest works of the ages before us—but who ever won anything who was afraid, or without faith. *We'll win.* (Refers to anti-vice work among soldiers)[74]

    Yesterday we tried out our high pressure canner at Wooldridge School—25 in club. some complications—lots of fun and experience

[72]Mrs. Fred Scott contributed a regular column on women's clubs and social activities to the *Austin American*. Her column of May 23 reports that the Austin suffrage group heard a report from Elizabeth Speer on the recent state convention in Waco and adopted a resolution presented by Anna Pennybacker to call special attention to the immoral conditions of training camps on the Mexican border. The women agreed to offer their help on voter registration day and elected new officers. Having served the maximum two terms, Jane McCallum was ineligible to serve again as president, and Mrs. Charles Haines was chosen to begin these responsibilities in October (*Austin American*, May 23, 1917, p. 8).
    [73]This is probably the Mrs. Doughty mentioned in McCallum's diary entry of June 12, 1918.
    [74]This parenthetical note was added after the main entry was written. The Texas Woman's Anti-Vice Committee was organized on June 5, 1917, with representatives from many state women's groups attending and Minnie Fisher Cunningham presiding. Their express purpose was to "wage an effective campaign for better moral conditions for our [military training] camps." They attempted to create "White Zones" around the camps from which prostitutes were barred (Minnie Fisher Cunningham, Chairman of the Texas Woman's Anti-Vice Committee, to Madam President, June 20, 1917, McCP, II).

Saturday carloads of boys from Camp Funston (Leon Springs) came in; Charles and Hubert among them. Mary Lee spent night out here, so she and Hubert took possession of seat under pergola; and K[athleen] and Charles of one by garden. Both boys appeared bright and early Sunday morning and remained for dinner and until time to journey back. They are certainly being put through, but are taking it like men.

[Pages have been torn out at this juncture, but there is no evidence that part of the diary has been deleted. The pages may have contained Henry McCallum's school work.]

June 15, 1917

During these troublous times of Kaiserism abroad, and would-be Kaiserism at home[,] one has no time to tell of events. On *ladies day* for sale of liberty bonds Mr Wroe[75] went half the day with Miss Lillie Robertson, her niece & me. In the aft.[ernoon] Miss L and I went alone. All told we sold \$5450[00] worth of bonds, and *learned lots*—there are many *different* brands of patriotism.

Wednesday last I had called meeting of suffragists and we went to work. American National, to my surprise, working with us—they are supposed to be violently opposed to suffrage.[76]

All told Wednesday I attended *five* meetings and cooked three full, *good* meals. Mr. M. and I were on platform at W.[ooldridge] park during mass meeting to condemn acts of this "wild hyena" as one speaker termed the governor James E Ferguson. Mr. M's few remarks were *most* favorably received.[77] We left early as I had engagement to explain bonds to Labor union meeting. Well—I did it and talked to them beside. The vision of our boys in the trenches of France makes it possible to *do anything* that can help bring this turmoil to an end. Yesterday [I] sold bonds *all day long* after getting machinery started all over town by which

[75] In addition to being president of Austin's Chamber of Commerce, Hiram A. Wroe was a vice-president of American National Bank (*1918 Austin City Directory*, 450). Suffragists in Austin followed the lead of the national organization in giving their whole-hearted support to the Liberty Loan campaigns. In all there were five such bond drives to finance the war between June 1917 and the Victory Loan of April 1919 (Richard B. Morris, ed., *Encyclopedia of American History* [New York, 1953], 1:277).

[76] American National Bank's stance on suffrage was irrelevant to the sale of liberty bonds. Its president, George Littlefield, was a major subscriber to the bonds, and the bank itself handled bond sales of over \$500,000 (*Austin Statesman*, June 15, 1917, p. 3).

[77] About 500 enthusiasts attended this anti-Ferguson rally. Mayor A. P. Wooldridge led off the speeches, which urged citizens to attend a meeting scheduled for the following Saturday, June 16, in Dallas to discuss "taking the University of Texas out of politics" (*Austin American*, June 14, 1917, p. 1).

dozens of women sold bonds. Wound up in Red Cross parade—most blistered—and I *know* my face was dirty—Got home to learn that Council of Presidents had all arrangements made for me to represent them in Dallas[78]—and to Dallas I go—fifteen rahs!! Oh, if only Ferguson can and will be impeached. He *deserves* to be hung for treason. *Think* of the lives that might be saved, by money we are compelled to spend to try to save our loved University from his—but not having the vocabulary of a sea captain, and being partly responsible for the respectability of my family, I can't express what I think of Jim Ferguson.

July 7, 1917

How can I ever remember even half the things I should like to record. The meeting at Dallas was what a Texan reporter would call a "humdinger." Can just jot notes to make me remember. For instance[,] the service car man charging Mrs Will Hart[79] and me only half fare to show sympathy with "what we were there for" (we had on badges)[.] The man insisting on furnishing a *stenographer and horrors*—neither of us had ever given dictation! The speeches, the crowds—the hot agony over which report to vote for—oh it was great![80]

Sunday morning when [I] arrived home found Mary Lee here, and [a] little later Hubert arrived for several hours—his parents moved here now. I donned my kimona, and stretched on the living room couch[;] talked myself hoarse to them all.

Monday brought reminder of work again—got some high school girls to help me on my committee for Dr. Noble's lectures[81] and we folded,

[78]Jane McCallum attended the Dallas assembly as a representative of the Council of Presidents of school Mothers' Clubs of Austin, forerunners of today's Parent-Teacher Associations (*Austin Statesman*, June 17, 1917, sect. 2, p. 4).

[79]Carrie Hart was the wife of attorney William D. Hart (AF - Biography, James Pinckney Hart (2), AHC, APL; *1918 Austin City Directory*, 254).

[80]The event which triggered this loud cry from all corners of the state and resulted in the Dallas meeting was Ferguson's veto of nearly the whole appropriation for the University of Texas for the biennium. About two thousand people from three-fourths of the counties in Texas (including about 300 from Austin) met from 10:00 A.M. until 6:00 P.M. on June 16. Two reports were presented by the Committee on Resolutions. The minority report called for Ferguson's impeachment. The other, which prevailed in the end, pleaded for the continued, uninterrupted functioning of the university: to make the group a permanent campaign to save the university and promote a state constitutional amendment to remove it from politics, to condemn the governor's actions, and to seek legal means to restore the appropriation. Those supporting the successful resolutions had nothing good to say about Governor Ferguson, but argued that the group's purpose should be to work for the university and not to embroil it in a prolonged political battle (*Austin American*, June 17, 1917, pp. 1, 2, 3).

[81]Mary Riggs Noble, M.D., gave a series of lectures, sponsored locally by the YWCA, on "Woman's Social Responsibility in War Times" (*Austin Statesman*, June 19, 1917, p. 5).

addressed[,] stamped and sent out literature and otherwise worked up crowd. Got Mr. Merrill (acting principle [of] Summer school) to dismiss [the] girls for 3 successive mornings she'll be here. I introduced her to girls Wed. A.M. but could not go back as [a] call came Thursday to report for Red Cross collections. It was *some* work,—will put in clippings. Don't understand quite how my committee came out next to head of the nineteen when so many others had own cars, and plenty of servants etc. The weather was the hottest, and dryest, and dustiest I most ever felt, but as Alvaro writes about wheat fields "we should worry!" I'm sure *nothing to drink* in life will ever look as tempting and taste as unspeakably good as did the ice tea Mrs. Vinson saved us from perishing with. We learned of *lots* of *different kinds* of patriotism. Wish I had time to write some of our experiences down.

Poor sister Penn has taken the presidents to task for sending *me* to Dallas instead of a president.[82] Life would lose some of its most amusing features if I didn't have her to laugh at, but she surely makes lots of people hate her.

I got away from serious things Monday, and chaperoned a Phi Gam dance; and really had a *lovely* time. It is good to laugh so much once in a while, and the antics of some of those boys were killing. Their search for needle & thread to sew ripped sleeve in Evelyn's dainty white dress, their frantic efforts (all put on) to keep E[velyn] & I from seeing in their cyclone struck appearing rooms, then their triumphant expression as they (Gabe Allen & Kurt Beckman) at last brought me some number 30 black thread and a rusty spike of a darning needle! At my suggestion that they *must* have white thread Kurt replied "No, we dont sew up holes in *white* ones—they dont *show* you know." There were about eight Aviators[83] present and it was hard to keep down the heart-ache as I talked to and looked at their fine young faces and realized—what? Talked to Grant Brush, now an officer[,] a long time. also to Rex Shaw. They both leave on fifteenth for service. Grant an only child. As I was [the] only chaperone I was treated beautifully—brought me *three saucers of cream.*

Went to Mr. Stockards and Miss Jonnie Magees wedding night before last;[84] to dinner with Mae and some of her friends last night and to

[82]Ada Penn (Mrs. Robert L.) was active in the Mothers' Clubs of Austin and the Council of Presidents (*Austin American,* May 15, 1917, p. 8).

[83]The aviators were probably uniformed students at the School of Military Aeronautics. See Part 3, n42.

[84]Jonnie Megee was a teacher at Austin High School before her marriage. LeRoy V. Stockard was in the Texas Department of Education until he became principal of Austin High School in 1917 (*1916 Austin City Directory,* 315; *1918 Austin City Directory,* 405).

Mothers complimentary concert at Wooldridge Park; afterward to help mothers seat singers for community singing. Dr. Geo. Butte made splendid talk under trying and occasionally *crying* circumstances— thousands of children—estimated crowd of 7000.[85]

During first part of July Evelyn Chumney spent week with Kathleen, Robert & Hal Miller from San Marcos spent two days with boys and Mary Lee came by from S.[an] A.[ntonio] and spent day and night. She and H.[ubert] had straightened out their affairs I'm thankful to say.

Attended July 10, what might be termed the culmination of a city hall romance. Mayor Wooldridge and Mrs. Holden—Charities Sec.[retary]— were married at her home.

July 1917

Yesterday I came near being "counted out." First, no servant appeared. Then I had the material for our Suffrage corner (I am so proud of recently getting in Austin American)[86] to prepare and send down; then Dr. Mather 'phoned for me to get ten or twelve women to meet as many men so we might merge the two anti-vice leagues[87]—as we had planned previously; then chairman of Hoover pledge cards[88] 'phoned to have us—suffragists—take charge Saturday and I had to get committee for that, then our State President unexpectedly arrived and Miss Gearing[89] and she 'phoned me to come have lunch with them and discuss *these problems*, but I had to get dinner & do things mentioned, but was going after dinner, but Kath[leen] got *real* sick, and fainted on my hands when I put her in a tub of hot water. After I got her out—with mamma's help—

[85] The *Austin American* chastised the city and the crowd for their "unnecessary noises" which prevented many from hearing the concert. At the time, Dr. George C. Butte, whose speech was entitled "Patriotism in the Home," was on the law faculty at the University of Texas (*Austin American*, July 7, 1917, p. 4).

[86] Jane Y. McCallum's weekly "Suffrage Corner" first appeared in the *Austin American* on July 1, 1917, and continued until February 1918, about the time the primary suffrage bill was introduced in the legislature.

[87] The men's and women's anti-vice leagues merged under the presidency of Dr. W. T. Mather, with McCallum serving as first vice president (*Austin American*, July 25, 1917, p. 3).

[88] The pledges given to Herbert Hoover, then U.S. Food Commissioner, were to conserve food in the home and to follow the directives of his office. The version published in McCallum's "Suffrage Corner" asked Hoover, in return for the women's pledges, to use his influence to secure early submission of the equal suffrage issue to Congress. This is only one of the ways in which women's war work and woman suffrage were intertwined (*Austin American*, July 29, 1917, p. 12).

[89] A leader in the national movement to develop home economics as a subject in higher education, Mary E. Gearing established the department at the University of Texas and served as its first chairman. The department conferred its first degree in 1917 (*Austin American*, May 11, 1946, p. 1).

who, thank goodness, has come home—I was simply done for until this morning, but got up to get breakfast at 5.40 and wound up with anti-vice meeting at Y.M.C.A. Mr. M. is turning out lights on me so will tell of this meeting later. Also must tell of party at Ellises, and of Aviators out Sunday, and of how I met them—By the [way] have left out about conscription etc. *must* put that in—parade etc.

Mr. Powell, acting mayor while Mr. Wooldridge is away on honeymoon—'phoned me to help select some women to meet at his office and arrange to boost conscription. Had very successful meeting, but of course, as always happens to those who can't say no, was put chairman of committee on womens—or girls—part of parade—and at Mr. Longs (Sec[retary] of Chamber of Commerce)[90] request, [I was] made his *assistant* in publicity, banners etc.

Parade with Besserers band leading, then nearly two hundred aviators (stationed at training camp here) then my girls—a hundred[,] papers state—then boy scouts—bless their hearts. I had had a com.[mittee] meeting night before, but sat up until nearly twelve afterward to try to work out some mottos for banners[.] I did my best, and sent designs to Mr Long at 6.30 next morning so he could have them painted. Then they were used on the nine automobiles Mrs. Goeth[91] and I [had] gotten to go out and parade. I was too busy to go down, but after all that, I've never *seen* the banners! When I asked for them for [the] girls to carry they were not to be found. Mrs Goeth was worried to death but we went along without them and learned afterward that the man Mrs G told to give them to either Mr. Long or me had put them in Lieutenant Sheltons car, and that poor man was having such a time trying to get the *undrilled* girls to parade like the soldiers that he *forgot the banners.*—the *point* to our part.[92] The speaking was on [Congress] Avenue, and such a sea of faces—all seemingly masculine and between 21 and 32. At the last minute they wanted *me*[,] just fancy, *me* to make a speech, and when I refused, then they asked me to get a number of women and sit on

[90]The parade on July 10 was intended to promote enlistment in the Texas National Guard. Sixteen thousand men were needed. Walter E. Long's tenure as secretary of the Chamber of Commerce was a remarkable thirty-five years (*Austin American*, July 12, 1917, p. 2; Humphrey, *Austin*, 228).

[91]Julia Tips Goeth was very active in civic affairs and club work. She was a member of the Austin School Board when this was written (AF - Biography, Goeth family, AHC, APL).

[92]McCallum's charges in the parade included University of Texas sorority members, women's club ladies, and suffragists. Horace Shelton, who had been appointed an officer in the state guard by Governor Ferguson, presided over the patriotic speech making (*Austin American*, July 12, 1917, p. 2).

platform. Mrs. Miller[,] Virginia [Miller], Marion Hawkins and Emily Rice were the first I found so we did our best. As we were coming home some aviators were coming down [the] street, and rather timidly but mischievously saluted our caps[.] 3 of us had on flag caps. As they looked at me one said right low "who is the goddess of Liberty?" and what should Mrs. M.[iller] do but say "Wait and I'll introduce you!" *Sure they waited*—I've mentioned *the girls*; and she asked their names and introductions followed. It was according to the spirit in which we are treating them and they appreciated it very much. They came on home with us, and I never saw such gratitude as when we invited them to our homes. (The invitation to mine was accepted *first* Sunday following by Messrs Rowell & Johnson)

It was pitiful to hear of their disillusioning when in patriotic ardor they volunteered—without waiting for *officer's* training camps or *any* thing—and were rushed to Camp Kelly to realize that in San Antonio the uniform *is not* even *respected*, and that any little effort toward the right sort of companionship was snubbed. Not a *respectable* woman spoke to them in their 3½ months in S A. Being college men, of good families it seemed unreasonable to them, and, in comparison, they declare Austin seems like Heaven. I reminded them that being a post town, S. A. is accustomed to the ordinary *peace time* private in the regular army who doesn't respect himself, and whom no girl could possibly risk being even kind to. They, of course, can't understand why they can't make the distinction, but they are making brave, and somewhat successful attempts (—Gee—Mary Helen Holden came to tell the boys something about where they are to sleep—they sleep there on account of insurance while the bride's away[93]—Charles [Freeman] 'phoned from Camp Funston to *says its raining there and he's lonesome*, Arthur and some boys came in, then Arthur and a girl to play K's eukalalie(?) she wont let them take off; and two people have telephoned—all since I commenced writing this)

The McCallums' hospitality to the aviators was remembered in this note, dated September 1, 1917.

My dear Mrs. McCallum —

Owing to the early and rather abrupt departure which I was required to make when at Austin, I remember that I was almost too excited to more

[93]Among the interruptions to writing in her diary, McCallum apparently received word that Mary Helen Holden wished "the boys" to occupy her mother's house while her mother, now Mrs. A. P. Wooldridge, was on her honeymoon.

than express a hasty good-bye to you—Allow me to say therefore that I shall never forget my all but too short acquaintanceship with you and Kathleen and I sincerely hope that, should the opportunity arise again, that I might enjoy another visit to Austin and in reality learn to know you better. I appreciate the fact that during my short stay in Texas as an aviation student I was privileged to meet a number of wonderful Austin people as well as to become acquainted with the town—to be sure, Austin is pleasant enough, as much of it as there is—but it does not nearly do justice to the magnanimity of its people. . . .[94]

Jane McCallum's handwritten notation on this letter reports that the author was "Killed in action" during the war.

[The July 1917 entry continues.]
The Ellis party was delightful, but oh, so sad sad when one stopped to think. He has been fired by those brewery hounds of regents. The party was a farewell to the Kelleys[95] who are leaving before being muzzled or fired and most of [the] guests were fine, brainy men—University men—who are in the most humiliating positions. It may be wicked, but how delighted, and supremely happy we'd all be if Ferguson, Littlefield, Allen, Fly and McReynolds were to be killed.[96]
Oh, I *can't* tell of all this anti-vice work—University work, Hoover pledge work—but after [a] meeting last night at Y.M.C.A. old *Judge Townes*[97]—bless his heart—brought me home in his electric [car] and talked a half hour afterward. (As I told him, he is a dead game sport. Not *an inch* is he giving to keep them from firing him. Says he could never again look those hundreds of young lawyers he has helped train in the face.[)] I never dreamed a human being could think on so low a plane as

[94]Joseph F. Wehner to JYM, Sept. 1, 1917, personal and business folder, McCP, II.
[95]Truman L. Kelley was a professor of the philosophy of education (*1916 Austin City Directory*, 279). His wife is mentioned in the diary entry for Nov. 2, 1916.
[96]George Littlefield, a university regent since 1911, generally supported Ferguson. Wilbur P. Allen of Austin was among Ferguson's appointees in January 1917. He was elected chairman of the board of regents at their spring 1917 meeting. Dr. A. W. Fly, appointed a regent by former Governor Oscar Colquitt yet an ally of Ferguson's, was a physician and former mayor of Galveston. Dr. G. S. McReynolds of Temple, also a Colquitt appointee, resigned from the board of regents while under fire from Ferguson in June 1917 (*Austin American*, Apr. 25, 1917, p. 1; *Handbook of Texas*, 1:613; H. Y. Benedict, comp., *A Source Book Relating to the History of the University of Texas* [Austin, 1917], 835-36).
[97]John Charles Townes was dean of the University of Texas law school from 1907 to 1923 (*Handbook of Texas*, 2:792).

University State regent McReynolds who said to Judge *Townes* words to this effect, "You University professors are the ones to blame for its (University) being in politics. You vote and *you've no business to.* Its *there* you get it [the university] in politics because you don't often vote for the man who wins, and of course the one who does *has it in for you* and the University— you ought not to vote."

Who can *think* of such a thing without almost bursting with rage! I have Judge T's word for it. Think the old man's coming for suffrage. He said in his humorous—*I will be cheerful* way that we'll decide our nine year old controversy as to which will play Beauty and which the Beast and put this play on to make a living.

Was called to Miss Gearings this P.M. where she, Mrs. Cunningham (State Pres[ident of] Suff[rage association]) Mrs Speer & Mesdames Ellis & Pearce[98] & I made all sorts of plans to see what women can do in University affair—More anon.

What the women could do in the University affair proved to be a great deal. The friends McCallum listed in her diary entry were the organizers of a public demonstration which transfixed the city of Austin for an entire summer day in 1917. Perfect in its timing, the rally focused attention on Governor Ferguson's misdeeds before an audience which encompassed farmers, legislators, students, and suffragists. Although questions concerning Ferguson's bank loans and his honesty had been raised in the state Senate, speakers at the women's rally no doubt placed heavier emphasis on his interference in university affairs.

Tension between the University of Texas and Governor Ferguson dated almost from the day the governor took office in 1914.[99] In his eyes, public funds were being lavished on the elitist state university in Austin to the neglect of rural schools and the Agricultural and Mechanical College in College Station. The controversy had intensified considerably since the fall of 1916, as Ferguson increasingly sought to impose his will on the board of regents in selecting a university president, dismissing faculty members, determining faculty work loads, and controlling spending. With the resignation of one regent in

[98]Belinda Pearce's husband James E. Pearce was principal of Austin High School from 1896 to 1917, when he joined the anthropology department at the University of Texas (AF-Biography, J. E. Pearce, AHC, APL).

[99]This discussion is drawn largely from Lewis L. Gould, "The University Becomes Politicized: The War with Jim Ferguson, 1915-1918," *Southwestern Historical Quarterly*, 86 (Oct. 1982): 255-76 and Gould, *Progressives and Prohibitionists*, 185-221.

the fall of 1916 and the expiration of the terms of three more in January 1917, Ferguson appointees and allies comprised a majority of the governing board.

The pace of developments quickened in late spring. On May 28, 1917, McCallum's acquaintance, George Peddy, led a large group of University of Texas students and ex-students in a noisy rally at the capitol. The anti-Ferguson crowd launched a publicity campaign to refute the governor's charges of extravagant spending, fiscal irregularities, and elitism. Meanwhile, faculty members appealed—without success—to the courts for aid in blocking the regents' efforts to remove them.[100]

When the governor vetoed nearly the entire university appropriation in early June, talk of impeachment became louder, particularly among the school's boosters. Their organizational meeting in Dallas, which Jane McCallum attended, gave a formal voice to their protestations. Meanwhile, Ferguson fanned the flames of the dispute in speeches to his rural constituents.

The ultimate insult to the university was delivered at the regents' meeting on July 12 and 13. As Ferguson wished, the board fired Professors L. M. Keasbey (institutional history), W. T. Mather (physics), William H. Mayes (journalism dean), R. E. Cofer, G. C. Butte (both law), and A. Caswell Ellis (philosophy of education), and university secretary John Lomax. Regents George Littlefield, W. G. Love, C. E. Kelley, and John M. Mathis voted in favor of the dismissals, joined on one or two occasions by chairman Wilbur P. Allen. The three other regents—W. R. Brents, Fred W. Cook, and Dr. S. J. Jones—opposed the firings.[101] Judge John C. Townes, dean of the law school, and Judge William S. Simkins, professor of law, were notified within several days of the session that motions on their dismissal had been tabled until the October meeting.[102]

Near the end of July, House Speaker F. O. Fuller called a special session of the legislature for August 1 to consider impeachment of Governor Ferguson. Austin during the last week of July was also the scene of the annual Farmers' Institute, when farming families from throughout Texas assembled to learn about new agricultural methods

[100]*Austin American*, July 5, 1917, p. 1.

[101]*Austin American*, July 14, 1917, p. 1. All the regents but Littlefield and Cook had been appointed by Ferguson. Love and Mathis, however, were participating in the meeting without having been confirmed by the Texas Senate (Benedict, comp., *A Source Book*, 835-36).

[102]*Austin American*, July 18, 1917, p. 1.

and exchange information. While Ferguson may have seen the gathering as an opportunity to demonstrate his popularity, Austin women and others active in the campaign against him saw it as the perfect chance to put their views before the people.

Jane Y. McCallum wrote a vivid account of the events of July 28, 1917, for her chapter in Frank Carter Adams's *Texas Democracy*. With typical modesty, she omits mention of the fact that she was one of their primary organizers and promoters. Her membership in the Colonial Dames could well have been the link that encouraged women from several patriotic women's groups to participate.

Friends of higher education rushed to the capital city in response to the clarion call. Ferguson looked to rural residents for his chief support. In the midst of preliminaries to the legislative session called for "impeachment purposes," a "Farmer's Institute" attended by over two thousand farmers and their families assembled in the capitol.

The times were very exciting. In addition to the residential population, there were the senators and representatives, members of the tribunal before which the offending governor would have to give an account of his stewardship; hot-headed University students milling about, and kept in bounds only by calmer ex-students gathered in Austin by the hundreds; there were lawyers interested in the opposing sides; progressive farmers and their families; others from the forks of the creek; charcoal burners and wood haulers from the surrounding hills—wondering what it was all about; friends of the accused;—and everywhere, on the streets, in public buildings, guarding the governor, the capitol, the mansion, mingling with the crowds and noting every movement, were towering figures, shod with cowboy boots, covered with "Texas Stetson," and armed with honest-to-goodness guns. They were Texas rangers; said to have been summoned by the governor from the border and the "badlands" for his "protection."

In the midst of this perfervid, chaotic situation, women, who were friends of the State University and not particularly sympathetic toward the gentleman whose record was up for discussion, decided to take a hand.

Led by their State president, Mrs. Minnie Fisher Cunningham, the members of the Equal Suffrage Association had during preceding years built up a State-wide organization which was a marvel of efficiency. Ferguson probably had another name for it, in the light of later events and the remark of the expert stage-driver that "a fly is a fly and a leaf is a leaf, but a hornet's nest is an organization." By whatever name, this machine, which included in its files the background of every law-maker in the State capital, was brought to Austin and placed at the disposal of the committee, along with the services of a Woman's Committee.

"If only we might have an opportunity of placing the facts before the farmers they would never support Ferguson," was the committee's cry when the Farmers' Institute referred to was assembling.

It was when they were denied this opportunity, after announcement that "Farmer Jim" would address the farmers, that an ingenious method was devised by the women political leaders, joined by women patriotic organization leaders, of placing the facts before the public, especially the farmers whom Ferguson was using all of his wits to prejudice against their State school.

Secrecy was maintained as to their intentions, but they were observed to be hastening to sundry parts of town including the telegraph station and the habitats of orators, draymen, sign-painters, and city commissioners.

When morning dawned of the day "Farmer (?) Jim" was to address the Institute in the afternoon, early arrivals on Congress Avenue at 13th Street stared in wonderment. They rubbed their eyes and looked again. *"Women of Texas Protest."* It was no optical illusion. There it loomed on the corner of the city's main thoroughfare, right in front of the capital grounds and flanked on the West by a State Park.

The words blazed from two orange colored banners, eight feet long, that were attached to scaffolding on either side of a large dray, further embellished with orange and white bunting, colors of Texas University.

Continued observation disclosed a unique procedure: without intermission except for brief introductions by a feminine presiding officer,[103] one man and woman after another climbed on the dray and made a speech; not perfunctory talks, but addresses that were earnest, able, and in many instances impassioned.

While the proceedings were in charge of a younger set, an atmosphere of impressive dignity and implacable seriousness was furnished the occasion by a group of distinguished, gray-haired women who sat with the speakers on the improvised rostrum, quietly knitting for sons or grand-sons—"somewhere" on the battlefields of France. The regent for Texas of the Mount Vernon Association of America, Mrs. T. S. Maxey, sat between the president of the Colonial Dames of America in the State of Texas, Mrs. T. B. Lee, and a vice-president, Mrs. Caroline C. Price, of the

---

[103]Jane McCallum presided (*Austin American*, July 29, 1917, p. 11).

same conservative organization. Mrs. Joseph D. Sayers, wife of one of Texas best-loved, ex-governors, and Mrs. W. H. Bell were there, and others who, as the papers stated, "stand for the highest and noblest in America." For such well-known, ultra-conservatives to unite with the "modernists" in any public effort, was surprising; but to take active part with them in a spectacular sixteen-hour street demonstration of this character, partook of the incredible.

The gathering crowds pushed nearer to within sound of the voices of the speakers in their eagerness to learn what it was all about. They were not kept in doubt. From the brilliant and persuasive efforts of the son of a tenant farmer who had worked his way through "State," and the equally persuasive but more homely speech of the farmer girl graduate who left a basket of Elberta peaches she was preparing to preserve "to rotten on my back porch" in her hurry to come to the defense of her beloved *Alma Mater*, to the addresses of the older and more learned lawyers, business men and educators, the speakers with one accord were giving the unembellished, Simon-pure facts of the Ferguson administration. The farmers got the facts, and the crowd[,] because [the surrounding streets were] so dense with traffic[,] was blocked despite the commodious park to the side, and the "continuous protest" had to cease long enough to adjourn to the city's largest park where shortly before midnight it came to a rousing close with a speech by "fighting Bob Shuler," the well-known Methodist evangelist.[104]

[The diary entry dated July 1917 continues.]

While in town Mrs. Hamby told me of seeing Arthur do a wonderfully brave act at Deep Eddy in rescuing [a] *woman* from some of that peraphanalia.[105] When I told Arthur about it he simply said "oh shucks," and went bolting out of the room. I love to hear a thing like that—I hope I'll never have a child do a cowardly deed, or one that will boast of his brave deeds.

Had a really unusual experience while waiting for car. Saw a man "take it" when some one called—while looking at posted draft numbers—"they've got you spot."[106] Want to take time and tell of this right.

[104]JYM in Adams, ed., *Texas Democracy*, 474-76.

[105]Deep Eddy Bathing Beach, now Deep Eddy Pool, is located near Town Lake just west of Loop 1. In its early days the pool's paraphernalia included "slides, springboards, trapezes, flying rings, horizontal bars, diving towers, etc." (Austin Chamber of Commerce, *Deep Eddy Bathing Beach* [Austin, n.d.], p. [1], AHC, APL).

[106]The order in which men would be drafted had been determined by a national lottery. This man had probably seen that his registration number was among those near the top of the list (*Austin American*, July 20, 1917, p. 1).

[This rhyme is recorded in the composition book following the diary entry for July 1917.]

> A husky old Scot named Mc D.
> Swilled so much of his native whiskee
> That he lost all his nerve
> And his strength and his verve,
> And at last found himself up a tree.
>
> The dame of this Scotchman Mc D.
> Was *not* a dissentor, you see
> So *she* took to strong drink
> Which bemuddled her think
> And to help him she cut down the tree.
>
> Another old Scot named Mc C[allum]
> Was hailed as the Scot[c]h Bonnee [or Bourree?]
> Tho an Elder in church
> He walked with a lurch
> And the way he could swear—holy Gee!
>
> In this gang there was one little Jane
> To whom all this boozing was pain.
> In their orgies erratic
> They dubbed her fanatic
> And she wished herself safely at hame.
>
> ~~But getting there couldn't be done~~
> ~~For the Scots were having their fun~~
>
> But getting there how could it be
> With the three on continual spree?
> Hist, she threw out the booze
> While they lay in a snooze
> And she found herself home in a jiffee[107]

Sat
Sept 1917
   "Hi—mamma—Mary Lee's stretched my pants so I can't wear em!"

---

[107]Jane McCallum is indulging in exaggeration in this ditty. Though "an Elder in church," Mr. McC was not a drinker (Editor's interview with Fritz McCallum, Frances McCallum, and Janet Poage, Mar. 6, 1986).

came in distressed tones from Brown a few minutes ago. In explanation[108] The Theta girls dressed as boys last night and acted as host escorts to the freshmen girls they are rushing. K[athleen] in Arthur's clothes made a charming boy. M.[ary] L.[ee] is here for rushing wk.

Nov. 2, 1917

It seems years instead of months since my last entry. At the present pace where can we land—but *my*, its interesting to live these days.

I almost reached my limit last August, so Mr. M. took me camping —

Dec.

Hubert and I almost pulled off a wedding—the only essential lacking being a bride! Pretty tough on the boy; but we took [a] long drive and talked it over and finally saw the humorous side to the extent that he laughed until he almost had to stop [the] car. M.[ary] L.[ee] went back to S.[an] A.[ntonio] with him. K.[athleen,] Charles [Freeman], Frank Buckner of Dallas & I went over Tuesday and I'll try to do trip justice when I'm not so *dead tired*. Visited Berta[109]—but as she said we came nearer entertaining her. Got there little past 1 o'clock. Lunched, talked, rested a little and Berta took K and me to call on some of our kin. K.[,] Chas.[,] Hubert & M. L. went to Mex[ican] restaurant for supper but B[erta] & I remained home to talk. Mrs. Dibrell saw K. & came out with John Danay to see me. Then the youngsters came & Berta met C. & H.[ubert] for first time. Being a graduate aviator Frank got passes for us all to go through Aviation fields (Kelley 1 & 2) and was to fly but we went to the wrong field first & got there too late to see him. We had to show our passes not only as we entered, but at

back to p 61

[The following is on hand-numbered page 61.]

every turn it seemed. I laughed so at the planes "getting a running start" & then running along like an immense sea fowl when they landed[.]

Hubert (now Captain on Colonel's staff) had invited us all out to dinner at officers headquarters. He got off in time to go around the immense camp (Travis) with us, and I *went into the trenches*; also into a *dug*

[108]"In explanation" was inserted after the sentence beginning "The Theta girls" had been written.
[109]Berta is Mrs. W. E. Smith (handwritten note on letter, Berta to JYM, Nov. 6, 1903, personal and business folder, McCP, II).

out camouflaged with growing shrubs, leaves etc. Saw the Boches[110] that are filled with straw instead of beer, and vulnerable parts plainly marked for bayonet practice. They *go at them* over the shell craters. The dinner was *good* & the company good. Enjoyed the Hostess House—not so sure of hostess herself. Went back to Bertas and started home not realizing that I'd had aught but a delightful time. On the way hom[e] a troop train, *crowded* to the rails passed us. *It was going East.* That night I slept scarcely three hours, and *then* I saw our boys in those terrible trenches

[110]The term "Boches" was used disparagingly to refer to Germans. Roughly translated, it means "cabbage heads."

PART 3

WINNING THE VOTE

During much of 1917 the energies of Texas suffragists were diverted toward winning the war on the home front and waging battle against Governor Ferguson. Yet they seldom missed an opportunity to remind the public of their ultimate goal.

As a journalist, Jane McCallum could reach a sizable Austin audience and help keep the suffrage issue alive. Shortly after her return from the anti-Ferguson meeting in Dallas, she was moved to write a letter (excerpted below), dated June 27, 1917, to the editor of the *Austin American*.

In her letter McCallum attempted to dissociate the majority of suffragists from the more militant National Woman's Party which had broken off from the National American Woman Suffrage Association. The Woman's Party, under the leadership of Alice Paul, held the Democratic party responsible for blocking the federal suffrage amendment and was actively anti-Wilson. In addition, members had agreed not to take part in war work as a group. Their activities focused solely on the federal suffrage amendment. The women held parades, demonstrated, picketed, spent time in jail, and generally behaved in what McCallum regarded as an unladylike manner. In part, McCallum's letter responded to the *Austin American's* front page coverage of recent arrests of members of the National Woman's Party who had been picketing the White House. The desire to distance themselves from this group was a part of the reason she noted, "we called ourselves 'suffrag*ists*,'" not suffragettes.[1]

[1]The Russian banner incident, an attempt to embarrass Wilson, who was host to a visiting Russian delegation, took place on June 20, 1917. Picketers were first arrested on June 22 (Christine A. Lunardini, *From Equal Suffrage to Equal Rights: Alice Paul and the National Woman's Party, 1910-1928* [New York, 1986], 20, 25, 110, 114-17; *Austin American*, June 23 and 26, 1917, p. 1; handwritten note in JYM's copy of Willie D. Bowles, "History of the Woman Suffrage Movement in Texas" [M.A. thesis, University of Texas at Austin, 1939], Series BA, McCallum Papers, Part I, Austin History Center, Austin Public Library [hereafter cited as McCP, I]).

Editor Austin American:

I shall attempt to give you some faint idea of how grieved and indignant suffragists here feel over the moving-picture spectacle now being enacted in Washington by a certain group of women.

In the first place we shall be deeply grateful if you, editorially, will remind the reading public that these women, whose chief occupation in this soul-trying period, seems to be that of attracting undesirable notoriety to our cause, do not belong to the National Association of Suffragists at all.

Being decidedly radical in their views and hopelessly in the minority in their numbers they broke away from the National because of what they term our "conservatism," and organized themselves into "The Woman's Party." . . .

[T]he great majority of American suffragists are doing [war work] out of pure patriotism and without parade or ostentation, as a matter of course.

Can it be possible that the men, in whose power lies the authority to grant to women that their opinions be counted, will allow themselves to be influenced by this little group of paraders in Washington, D.C.?[2]

In her weekly "Suffrage Corner" McCallum had comparatively free rein to promote the suffrage issue. The following excerpts, which appeared in the *Austin American* during the fall of 1917, demonstrate her lively journalistic style and give one a taste of the rhetoric of the woman suffrage campaign.

Every few days some one telephones just to state that they are going in for suffrage this fall. It may seem incredible, but they usually seem to be of the opinion that there are political and educational tangles in Texas that the men need assistance in straightening out.[3]

Again we ask: Why should one consider the women who picket the white house representative of the women of the country, any more than they consider the I.W.W.'s representative of the men of the country?[4]

[2]Newspaper clipping, Series H, #1, McCP, I. Ellipses delete McCallum's references to the National Woman's Party's unsuccessful efforts in behalf of Republican presidential candidate Charles Evans Hughes and the Russian banner incident and her list of women's contributions to the war effort.

[3]*Austin American*, Sept. 9, 1917, p. 5.

[4]*Austin American*, Sept. 30, 1917, p. 12. The Industrial Workers of the World was a

Have you ever during a leisure moment perused an authentic ... "list of persons excluded from suffrage [in Texas]?" ... Idiots, lunatics, felons, United States soldiers, marines and seamen, women.

It is evident that Texas women should be overcome with gratitude to those self-proclaimed chivalrous gentlemen, wherever found, who, with oratory and panegyrics[,] seek to save us from association with the men considered intelligent and law-abiding enough to have a voice in their own government, while they consign us to the above enumerated delectable (barring soldiers, marines and seamen) society.[5]

After Tuesday's election object lesson, surely no thinking or consistent Austin man will ever again advance as an argument against suffrage that "women wouldn't use it if they had it." ...

[S]carcely more than one-third of the 3500 [eligible male voters] took the trouble to go to the polls.

This is not intended as an expression for or against the bond issues, and the purchase of Barton Springs, but as an expression of absolute astonishment that men can be so indifferent regarding the outcome of issues of such vital importance.

We presume they are getting tired of the vote![6]

At the annual convention of the National American Woman Suffrage Association, held in Washington, D.C., in mid-December 1917, President Carrie Chapman Catt urged delegates to visit their congressmen and ask them to vote for the woman suffrage amendment to the Constitution.[7] The U.S. House of Representatives had scheduled a vote on the amendment for early January 1918, the outcome of which would to a large degree determine the agenda of the Austin Equal Suffrage Association for the year.

In late December, the Texas suffrage organization was gathering signatures for a petition to Congress, as McCallum reported in her diary.

[The misdated entry below follows chronologically the material on page 61 in the diary.]

revolutionary industrial union. Its antimilitaristic stance and disruptive strikes during the First World War were considered treasonable by many Americans (*Dictionary of American History*, rev. ed. [New York, 1976], 3:412-13).

    [5]*Austin American*, Oct. 7, 1917, p. 19.
    [6]Ibid.
    [7]*Austin American*, Jan. 6, 1918, p. 12.

Dec 20, 1914 [1917] [8]

This may not be the "end of a perfect day" but it is of *some* busy one. Arose at 6 o'clock, got my family fed and off to school[,] commenced working E 5th Street for Red Cross members at 9.30 [—] got only 12, but my partner, Mrs. Chas. Glass[,] got only 3 and at Headquarters [they] said mine largest number turned in today (1 day)—others [had] been working all week. reason. Mrs Creighton met me & at 12.30 we had lunch at Y.W.[,] then started getting signers to *suffrage memorial* to Cong.[ress] sent by Mrs. Cunningham. We were very successful only *H. A. Wroe, Sam Sparks* & Gov. Sayers refusing.[9] *Latter* good suffragist *but queer notions.* I got the sigs signatures[10] off to Mrs C[unningham] and came home and wrote my suffrage corner, and if I was not so happy over $50.000 school bonds carrying by over 4 to 1 would be all in. Jesse here until Sat noon. Surely enjoy youngster. K.[athleen] being worked to a finish in aviation preperations Alvaro planning deer hunt.

[The following entry is misdated, given the events McCallum mentions and its appearance in her diary following the Dec. 20 entry.[11]]

Dec [Jan.] 8, 1918
10.45 P.M.

Just finished signing my name several hundred times as Sec.[retary] of Womans Com.[mittee] for prohibition for Austin.[12] Mrs. Gay[13] Ch.[airman,] Mesdames *Doom*, Creighton and I got a lot of letters sent to

[8]Clearly, McCallum misdated this entry. The school bonds were approved on December 20, 1917 (*Austin Statesman*, Dec. 16, 1917, p. 11).

[9]For H. A. Wroe see Part 2, n75. Sam Sparks was president of the Austin Chamber of Commerce and president of Texas Trust Company of Austin. Joseph Sayers was governor of Texas from 1899 to 1903 (*1918 Austin City Directory*, 309, 450; *Handbook of Texas*, 2:576).

[10]The explanatory word, "signatures," and the cryptic "reason." (above) were inserted at a later time.

[11]The "8" of 1918 is superimposed over the year 1917 for this entry. Most likely the month should be January, as McCallum refers to chaperoning a New Year's Eve party, petitioning congressmen, and the prohibition campaign.

[12]Several hundred Austin women had organized a women's drive or women's committee to work for the city prohibition referendum scheduled for Jan. 21. Leila (Mrs. J. B.) Gay served as general chairman and McCallum as secretary (*Austin American*, Jan. 9, 1918, p. 1). McCallum is listed as a member of the Austin Woman's Christian Temperance Union in a directory which postdates 1922 (Austin Woman's Christian Temperance Union, *Directory and Cookbook* [n.p., n.d.], 9). Since her diaries do not mention attending meetings between October 1916 and December 1919, she was probably not then a member of this group.

[13]Leila Gay was active in her church and was elected to the Austin School Board in 1917 (Moreland, *Texas Women*, 153-54; *Austin American*, Apr. 10, 1917, p. 8).

our *mis*-representative *Buchannon* and to Daniel Garret[t][14] about federal suffrage amendment. Amusing tilt with the governor. Mayfield[15] signed [the letter to Buchanan] like a pretty boy.

K.[athleen is] back in University. If only the boys will let her alone. Its aviators now; but I'll admit some of them are dears. ✝ Was the only chaperone at [the] Theta watch party New Year's eve. All boys but 2 were aviators and I lost my heart to them [even] if they *are* Yankees. Especially lovely to me were the quartet K. and Mary Watson have gone with so much: Tom Warren, Carl Squier (from Detroit related to Gen[eral])[16] Ray Stevenson and Bob Pike)

Some of them have run as much of a race over K. as Joe Wehner and the red headed May boy did last Summer. Lieutenant Marlowe mad because of confusion of dates.

Alvaro is going to radio night school in Univ.[ersity][17] tho rules say none under 20. He is 18 in Feb!

Consternation at American office. Compliments on my parody on Service[']s *Mud of Flanders* [see below] published and sent out by prohibitionists. Letter from Hubert telling of promotion from Colonel[']s to General's staff. [He] Was over last week.

Brown, K.[,] Henry & Alvaro all had roseola (Refuse to call it *German measles*.)

Robert Service's war poem is actually entitled "A Song of Winter Weather." McCallum's parody, reproduced here, identifies many of the anti-prohibitionists (the "wets") as disloyal German-Americans. She was particularly incensed that male German aliens who had merely applied for citizenship could vote on the prohibition issue,

[14]A former member of the Texas House of Representatives, James Buchanan represented the Tenth Congressional District from 1913 to 1933. Daniel Garrett was Congressman-at-large from Texas when this was written (*Handbook of Texas*, 1:235, 672).

[15]Earle Mayfield was a Texas railroad commissioner in 1917. He was elected to the U.S. Senate in 1922 after defeating James Ferguson in the primary and George Peddy in the highly controversial general election (*Handbook of Texas*, 3:582-83). For Mayfield's flirtation with the governorship, see McCallum's diary entries for July 3 and 4, 1919, and August 16, 1919, below.

[16]Major General George Squier was the U.S. Army's chief signal officer from 1917 to 1923 (Joseph G. E. Hopkins, ed., *Concise Dictionary of American Biography* [New York, 1964], 992).

[17]Since qualified radio operators were in short supply, the federal government requested that the University of Texas open a radio school. Those who had not yet been drafted were eligible to take the no-fee course, as well as men already conscripted (*Austin American*, Dec. 6, 1917, p. 4).

whereas she could not. McCallum's verse plays upon the marching rhythm of the original.

WOMEN WORKERS WOES

(With apologies to Rob't W. Service)

It isn't the "slackers" we fear;
It isn't the Sammies that fight;
It isn't the business career
Of our men, or political might;
We fear not the "loyal" who seek
To keep our place "wet" in the sun —
Its the brewery man
In the hands of the Hun —
        Its the Hun,
                Hun,
                        Hun.

It isn't the melee we mind.
That often is rather good fun.
It isn't the 'phoning we do,
Or dodgers disbursed by the ton;
It isn't the deafening[?] threats
From "antis" who really have souls,
Its the strafing we get
From the Kaisers own set —
        At the polls
                polls
                        polls

It isn't because we lack grit
That election days fill us with woes.
We don't mind a contest a bit,
If opposed by legitimate foes;
We're backing our boys "over there"
Prepared to meet measures most bold
But the Huns come to battle
Herding voters like cattle —
        Who've been sold
                sold
                        sold

Oh the Huns at the polls with the sold
The sold at the polls to the Hun;
While Americans say "We can't help it today" —
Then tomorrow — "Oh well, its all done!"
With never a vote to our names;
With men to our peril still cold;
Sure the worst of our foes
Is here at our doors:
    It's the Hun,
            at the polls,
                    with the sold.[18]

Austin suffragists' efforts to persuade Congressman J. P. Buchanan to vote for the federal woman suffrage amendment were futile, but President Wilson's endorsement on the eve of the vote gave the cause an enormous boost.[19] The amendment squeaked by the U.S. House of Representatives with barely the required two-thirds majority. When it finally came before the Senate in October, however, votes were wanting.

Jan 9, 1918
Dead tired, but happy! Worked prohibition and suffrage *all day* long until 5 P.M. Smoked old *Buchannan out* and busted suffrage treasury and all our friends wiring Washington.
Attended 2 pro[hibition] rallies, changed petition and —
Later —
Did I say tired? Never felt better in my life. Just heard from Mr. Walthall of [the] *American* that it has just come over wires *that Pres. Wilson has come out for Federal amendment.* Tired? Feel like I could walk to Washington just to give him a pat. *Can it really be true?*

In her "Suffrage Corner" column which appeared the following Sunday, Jane McCallum clarified the events of the suffragists' con-

[18]JYM, "Women Workers Woes," Series A.6, McCP, I.
[19]*Austin American,* Jan. 10, 1918, p. 1. The irony of Wilson's goal to "make the world safe for democracy" while women at home could not participate in American democracy was not lost on the suffragists. For an excellent discussion of this point, see Sally Hunter Graham, "Woodrow Wilson, Alice Paul, and the Woman Suffrage Movement," *Political Science Quarterly* 98 (Winter 1983-84): 665-79. The Texas Equal Suffrage Association made the identical argument in its call to convention in May 1917 (*Austin American,* May 6, 1917, p. 14).

frontation with Representative Buchanan.[20] Austinites had sent him a telegram which read, "In Texas a tide of resentment is rapidly rising against political conditions where we are bound to submit to a government that is participated in by other women, but from which our own women are barred."[21]

McCallum reprinted Buchanan's reply, dated January 9, 1918.

I am not convinced that a majority of Texas ladies desire the ballot. On the other hand, I am convinced that a majority of my constituents are opposed to national woman suffrage and it is my duty to reflect their will. Am further convinced that citizens of the south should oppose these amendments to the constitution that takes rights and powers from the state government and especially when such amendments give to the national government control of the domestic institutions of the state. I cannot support an amendment to the federal constitution enlarging the fifteenth amendment. It must be left to a younger generation than mine to repudiate the old ideals of the south.

(Signed) J. P. Buchanan, M.C.

The "Suffrage Corner" continues. Buchanan had apparently eluded the suffragists until, goaded by their telegram, he "got busy" and stated his position publicly.

All efforts at "smoking" out Congressman P.J. [sic] Buchanan had proved unavailing until the message he refers to [the suffragists' telegram above], with a dozen prominent signatures attached, was wired him. Then he got busy. So did the suffragists, and between thirty and forty "constituents" let him hear from them in no uncertain terms by return wire.

As some one remarked: "We've busted the suffrage treasury and many of our friends will have to declare a moratorium, but no representative or misrepresentative of ours in Washington can again look an honest person in the face and say "my constituents don't want it."[22]

[20]*Austin American*, Jan. 13, 1918, p. 4.
[21]McCallum is referring to the fact that by the end of 1917 women had full suffrage in twelve states and presidential suffrage in an additional four (Anne Firor Scott and Andrew Mackay Scott, *One Half the People: The Fight for Woman Suffrage* [Urbana, Il., 1975], 166-67).
[22]*Austin American*, Jan. 13, 1918, p. 4.

[The next diary entry refers back to these events of early January.]

Jan 21, 1918

It was true [that Wilson came out in favor of the suffrage amendment].
When news came over wires from Washington Bercowitz 'phoned from
[the] American for me to help get "expressions"[23] for paper next morning. Mrs. Fred Scott, Dr Eby[24] and I worked it and got 25 columns [,]
dandy ones.

Now, tonight I feel rather tense. It isn't quite 8 o'clock and the [Austin]
prohibition election *ballots are being counted.* Antis reported 109 ahead—
but our two best wards—3rd & 4th [still] to hear from and two bad
ones—5th & 7th. But hard work has been going on in them and am
hopeful. *Poor women who wait* (Mrs Gay & I as Chairman & Sec[retary] of
women workers signed our names *1000 times*[;] letter sent [to] that many
men)

> "Oh the madness,
> And the sadness
> And the gladness
> Of it all"

Last night was a blessed relief from the strain of work, and parade[25]
etc. etc. etc. *It never rains but it pours.* Sat afternoon at 5 o'clock we thought
today would be very quiet—no company. Then Bob Pike 'phoned he
wanted to bring his sister out to see K[athleen] & me & Carl Squier (Boys
keep phoning about election & oh joy we are 195 ahead)[26] broke in to ask
for date with K & to come tell me good-bye. Then M.[ary] L.[ee] 'phoned
[that] Hubert was on way over from S.[an] A.[ntonio;] then telegram
came to K. from Charles in Dallas that he was coming over! Such a stir,
as the one's coming to see K. were all due to arrive at about 7.30. To make

[23]The "expressions" were statements of gratitude to Wilson and to the Congressmen
who had passed the woman suffrage amendment. McCallum quoted herself as saying,
"My first emotion was naturally one akin to awe at the added responsibilities the ballot
will entail. . . . [O]ur splendid manhood will before long wonder that justice and release
for constructive work had not been given us long ago" (*Austin American*, Jan. 11, 1918, p.
2).

[24]Dr. Frederick Eby was a professor of the history of education at the University of
Texas (*1918 Austin City Directory*, 215).

[25]Woman's day for prohibition in Austin was celebrated by a parade up Congress
Avenue of more than 1,000 women, men, and children. It included University of Texas
coeds singing "The Eyes of Texas," servicemen, school children of all ethnicities, a band,
and banners reading "Vote Pro and Swat the Kaiser" and "No sugar for us, but the breweries get it" (*Austin American*, Jan. 20, 1918, p. 5).

[26]In the final tally, Austin prohibitionists won out by a margin of one hundred votes
(*Austin Statesman*, Jan. 22, 1918, p. 1).

long story short Charles train was six hours late so Carl & Bob and Miss Pike had gone before he got here. Hubert got in Sat night and was out most of Sunday with M.L.R. Was glad for him to meet the yankee boys & they all admired one another extremely—had told them each of the other. Before they came H.[ubert,] K & M.L. got on a tear—played uke, guitar & a *kazoo* H. brought out and I laughed *until I forgot*[.] When the others came they were rather sad over its being their last night but finally *partook* of the hilarious spirit of others and all had a jolly good time. I reiterate a previous statement—I did not know yankee boys *could* be so like our Southern boys. I shall always remember the motherless one, Carl Squier—who told me in such an appealing way how it made him realize more than ever what he'd missed when he met a woman he felt could have been such a *congenial chummy* mother. Wonder if my *own* will feel that way about me when they are his age? *If only they will!*

Haven't given the names of so many boy's [(]aviators[)] who've been out. As they come and go I'm so often reminded of the lines,

> "Ships that pass in the night
> And speak each other in passing —
> Only a signal shown,
> And a distant voice in the darkness.
> So on the ocean of life
> We pass and speak one another —
> Only a look and a voice
> Then darkness again — *and a silence*"[27]

We often bring them home with us from church and these are usually a different type from K's friends. One I invited because of his forlorn appearance turned out to be an artist and interesting—Beiser by name. I invited him to come back & bring a friend for Xmas dinner. He did—the friend Arnold from Oklahoma—Beiser is from N.Y. City. Two interesting ones—a socialist and a lawyer—Smith & Imes made things interesting one Sunday.

Jan. 23—1918

Lieutenant Marlowe who has almost annoyed K with his persistent attentions is downstairs saying good-bye preparatory to leaving tomorrow indirectly for France. He is what I've unconsciously pictured the typical yankee—and I don't care for him—Just different training per-

---

[27]The source of this familiar quotation is Longfellow's "Tales of a Wayside Inn, The Theologian's Tale, Part Third, Elizabeth IV" (*The Poetical Works of Longfellow*, Cambridge Edition [Boston, 1975], 274).

haps—and different blood from somewhere tho he declares his father is a Virginian—only mother yankee. He hails from Canton, Ohio.

Attended my first meeting today as member of State Suffrage Board.[28] Mrs. Frances Evans entertained us afterward at a lovely luncheon—in fact so *good* that it smacked of disloyalty!

While waiting together, Mrs. Moore—wife of Major Moore of *Pershing's staff*—gave me some of the most interesting bits of information I've heard. Major M. is Supt. of U.S. Army transport service in Europe is known as "the Man who is keeping France warm" and for his success in this assignment from "Gen Jack" has had his name sent in for full Colonel—skipping Lieutenant C.

The most touching story in real life centers around *not* the reward he got, but the reward he *wanted*. Will not write this down because cannot forget—Wish public could know about the *coal* conditions & they'd stop howling so of Garfields action.[29] Feb. 1940—Well—I *have* forgotten. How I wish I'd written it down.

The long interval between this diary entry and the next is evidence of the months Jane McCallum and others devoted to their work for passage of the primary suffrage bill. Their efforts began shortly after William P. Hobby assumed the governorship in September 1917 and continued until he signed the bill into law on March 26, 1918.

If women could vote in primary elections, they would essentially elect candidates to office, since Texas was a one-party state. Primary suffrage for women was also easier to obtain than full suffrage, since passage required only simple majorities in both legislative houses and the governor's assent. To achieve full woman suffrage meant amending the state constitution: winning two-thirds majorities in the legislature and approval by the voters.

At its January board meeting, which Jane McCallum attended, the Texas Equal Suffrage Association mapped out its strategy for the coming year. According to the notes of one board member, the group

[28]McCallum had been appointed to the board of the Texas Equal Suffrage Association in October 1917 as a committee chairperson (*Austin American*, Jan. 9, 1918, p. 8).

[29]As head of the Fuel Administration, Harry A. Garfield had ordered nonessential industries to operate on a limited basis between January 18 and 22, 1918, and for nine successive Mondays. The measure gave top priority to rail shipment of coal. Europe-bound ships docked on the East Coast were waiting for this vital commodity (Arthur S. Link, *American Epoch: A History of the United States Since the 1890's* [New York, 1955], 209-10; David M. Kennedy, *Over Here: The First World War and American Society* [New York, 1955], 123-25).

resolved to propose to Governor Hobby that, "if he will submit P[rimary] Suf[frage] at the special session & we secure the vote[s,] the Tex[as] Suf[frage] organization will use its influence & organization to assist him in his camp[aign] for Gov."[30]

Members of the group who lived in Austin assumed the major burden of the work for primary suffrage. A special legislative session would convene on February 26 to consider prohibition. The women lobbyists secured enough commitments from legislators to reassure Governor Hobby that a primary suffrage bill could pass. Perhaps feeling faint of heart, he instead submitted to the special session a primary election bill which provided for runoff elections and allowed the state Democratic executive committee to strike unqualified candidates from the ballot but omitted any mention of woman suffrage.[31] Charles B. Metcalfe, representative from San Angelo, introduced the primary suffrage bill as an amendment, and this passed the state House on March 16 and the Senate on March 21.[32]

Jane McCallum described the immediate aftermath of the Senate vote in her newspaper column the following Sunday.

A SCENE OF HISTORIC SIGNIFICANCE.

Minnie Fisher Cunningham is undoubtedly and unquestionably the woman of the hour and numberless hours to come in Texas.

When, on Thursday afternoon, the House concurred in Senate amendments to their bill giving women the right to vote in primaries and nominating conventions, the faithful little group of lobbyists rose, preparatory to leaving their long accustomed "suffrage corner" in the gallery.

Then it was that a scene was enacted that should go down in the pages of Texas history. The House membership, seeing them, rose and applauded vociferously and enthusiastically, crying "Speech! Speech!"

And here comes the eternal feminine touch: Instead of a triumphant, rather masculine—now that she is a voter—response, this strong and brilliant woman, realizing that the goal for which she has labored so faithfully and long was actually attained, trembled visibly, and, to use her own words, "never came so near collapsing" in her life.

[30]Addendum to letter JYM to Mrs. League, n.d., Series F.1, #301, McCP, I.

[31]Gould, *Progressives and Prohibitionists*, 234.

[32]JYM, in Adams, ed., *Texas Democracy*, 481; Nieuwenhuizen, "Minnie Fisher Cunningham and Jane Y. McCallum," 36-37, 38.

In Texas' hall of fame, in memory if not in actuality, a group portrait will hereafter appear, and it will bear the likenesses of Minnie Fisher Cunningham, Hortense Ward, Elizabeth Speer, Helen Moore, lobbyists who put suffrage over the top in Texas.[33]

Primary suffrage for women became law with Governor Hobby's signature, witnessed by Jane McCallum among others, on March 26. (See the diary entry for June 12.) Without an emergency clause, the law did not go into effect for ninety days—just seventeen days prior to the July primary. Hundreds of thousands of newly enfranchised Texas women would have little time to register to vote.[34]

Before registration had even begun, citizens of Austin and Travis County geared up to educate the new voters and formed the Good Government League. This group pledged to "participate in every campaign for the election of officers" and actively support responsible candidates. Jane McCallum was named vice chairman.[35]

Austin women worked feverishly to publicize the registration drive which opened on June 26. Procedures were outlined in the newspaper; there was friendly competition among the city wards over which would have the most registrants; Jane McCallum's "Women In Politics" column appeared frequently. To Nell Doom went the "task of 'dividing up the telephone book' so that no woman having a telephone can forget to register." When the books closed, 5,856 women were on the rolls for Travis County—about equal to the number of men expected to vote in the primary.[36]

5th
Sat. May ~~11th~~ 1918 [37]
Yesterday I sent to my department in the Statesman—*Woman and Her Ways*, what I termed "Leaves from the Log Books of Austin Women."[38]

[33]*Austin Statesman*, Mar. 24, 1918, sect. 2, p. 1.
[34]Nieuwenhuizen, "Minnie Fisher Cunningham and Jane Y. McCallum," 38.
[35]*Austin American*, Mar. 26, 1918, p. 4.
[36]*Austin Statesman*, June 23, 1918, p. 6; *Austin American*, June 27, 1918, p. 5; *Austin Statesman*, July 2, 1918, p. 5; *Austin Statesman*, July 15, 1918, p. 8.
[37]May 4 and 11, 1918, were Saturdays. McCallum's "Record" should therefore be dated Friday, May 3.
[38]McCallum's first "Woman and Her Ways" column appeared in the *Austin Statesman* on March 17, 1918. The "Leaves" were published in the column of May 5. The women were asked to choose a "typical, not an unusual" day to list their activities (*Austin Statesman*, May 5, 1918, sect. 2, pp. 1, 5).

It occurred to me to put down one of my own, but things went so fast I could not, and while trying to collect myself after my *sore* disappointment over Mamma & Mr. M. raising such cain that I had to give up the trip to Burnet to hear Ferguson fire his opening gun (to get points *against* him etc)[39] I'll put down what I can remember, so several things may be *left out*, but not a thing added.

~~Saturday May 4th 1918~~
Record for Friday May 4th 1918
(1) Rose at 5.30 to get Kathleen and Mary Lee off to Lampasas to appear before School Board (Laughed over their rehearsal of their speeches to ... [Board])
(2) Cooked their breakfast & served it to them
(3) Took Mamma's breakfast upstairs as she is not very well.
(4) Finished cooking b[reakfast] for rest of family.
(5) Put up a lunch for Alvaro.
(6) Found bushel basket for Brown to put potatoes in
(7) Wrote an hour on my newspaper stuff
(8) Got children off to school—sending work to Statesman by Arthur (Had answered 3 phone calls at intervals)
(9) Telephoned six people in response to request from Miss Jennie Burleson to get help at her booth.
(10) Cut out curtains for boy's room
(11) Had conversation concerning cow we think of buying
(12) Found such interesting material in mail about Woman's Oversea Hospital that wrote a lot more for paper.[40] (One phone call after the other)
    Letter from Dudley Woodward asking me to help him out on finding women speakers for Red Cross Drive—take it over while he is out of city for a week.
(13) Next door neighbor came in for about 20 minutes [—] looked at Cactus.
(14) Ordered groceries and meat and planned a *conditional* supper [—] 2 boys, Roger Harris & Skinner Bell to be here if came to track meet.
(15) Ate lunch.
(16) Soaked my *useless* feet while telephoning about war work

[39] Ferguson had declared his candidacy for the governorship. The state Democratic executive committee, still dominated by his supporters, voted to permit his name to appear on the ballot (Gould, *Progressives and Prohibitionists*, 238). Apparently, Jane McCallum's family felt that she had overexerted herself and forbade her making this trip.
[40] The Women's Oversea Hospital was operating under the auspices of the National American Woman Suffrage Association as part of its war work.

(17) Mrs. Daniels called in car, took me to Statesman, from where I went to Liberty Loan H'd'q at 2.35 to meet Mrs. Dave Doom.

(18) Worked all afternoon obtaining small subscribtions for $250^{00} pledge for State Suffrage.[41] People—*very* kind. Made it easier, as we *did mortally hate to do it* at *this time;* so twas helpful for them to say to us, as so many men did, "Always count me in." "No need to explain—when faithful workers like you ask for anything." "Don't care what its for—can't give much but good wishes with it etc etc"

(19) *Forgot to meet* with Mrs. Preston's committee at 3.30 we were so deep in above. (she has forgiven me & expecting her now to see me)

(20) Got home pretty tired, as had gone to bed at 12. the night before.

(21) Mr. & Mrs. J. A. Jackson came in after supper but seeing I had to go out, took me to Liberty Loan Hdqt's, where the men's Chairman, W. H. Richardson made the joyous announcement that we are over the top with more than our maximum!!!!!!!

'Phone call awaited me from Mrs. Jackson about how necessary she felt it was for me to go to Burnet today. So to bed at 11 oclock.

(One of the dozens of little things left out is what Mrs. Jackson told me about two soldier boys—no[,] instructors in S.[chool of] M.[ilitary] A[eronautics].[42] (1 in uniform 1 not) who live next door to us—Carl and Roscoe Runge

> Austin, Texas
> May 6, 1918

Mrs. Minnie Fisher Cunningham
1626 Rhode Island Ave
Washington, D.C.

Lunatics have troubles enough. Will do my best on program

> Jane

I'd thought I'd been through "kinder" busy days, but believe me—after sending above telegram in response to S.O.S. call from Mrs. C—to make out program for *State Suffrage* meeting here in Austin,[43] I found busy times before had merely been play.

[41]The Austin Equal Suffrage Association had pledged to raise $250 of the Texas quota of funds to sustain the Women's Oversea Hospital (*Austin Statesman,* May 9, 1918, p. 5).

[42]The School of Military Aeronautics, housed in the "Little Campus" at the University of Texas, was a ground school offering preliminary training to American airmen. It opened in May 1917 and closed in January 1919 (*Cactus: 1918* [Austin, 1918], 329; *Austin Statesman,* Jan. 31, 1919, p. 4; *Austin Statesman,* July 1, 1943, p. 18).

[43]The Texas Equal Suffrage Association convened in Austin, May 29-31, 1918 (JYM, in Adams, ed., *Texas Democracy,* 481).

June 12, 1918

This pretends to be something of a diary it seems, from glancing over it, and yet the occurrences of real *historic value* that have not even been referred to!

Why, Texas women are *voters* now; I helped lobby to make it possible; wrote—Mr. Metcalf[e] (our leader in the house) declares—most effectively to make it possible and was present when Gov. Hobby *signed the bill*. Others present were Mrs. Cunningham, of course, Mrs. Doom, Mrs Metcalf[e,] Mr. Metcalf[e] and Captain Sackett. The silver embossed pen was presented Mrs. C[unningham]—bless her heart—she certainly deserved a *crown*. I've been writing about primary suffrage so much—making so many speeches—*yes* think of it—*speeches* on suffrage, Hobby etc and trying so many things out that when time to write comes I am *exhausted*—as now. Made myself sick last winter selling thrift stamps on Vann Smith [Drug Company] corner two raw days.[44] Finally had to have 3 nose operations in one—bones that came out were the real thing—no gristle—had dental work done & was down and out several days, but back in time for 3rd Liberty Loan drive—government cards etc. Men held Kangaroo Court for those not coming across—painted Franz Fiset's premises yellow etc[45]—work & excitement a plenty

Kate brought Margaret[46] to be operated on for adenoids & tonsils. I stood by the child thro it all—didn't realize they go through with such *paroxysms* when under ether.

Hobby club *put over* by Mrs. Doom[,] Mrs Eby & self[47] (story herewith) now has membership of 1000 women who refused to second a motion at a Ladies Aid meeting two years ago, now making speeches for Hobby— Suffragists brought out Miss Blanton[48] against St[ate] Sup[erintenden]t.

[44] Van Smith Drug Company was on the corner of Congress Avenue and 6th Street (*1918 Austin City Directory*, 397).

[45] This was not an isolated incident. One manifestation of the anti-German sentiment of the times was ridiculing German-Americans who had not purchased sufficient Liberty Bonds by painting their homes yellow. See Leuchtenburg, *Perils of Prosperity*, 44. In Palestine, Texas, a "slacker" himself was painted, according to the *Austin American* (June 30, 1918, p. 9). Fiset was an attorney (*1918 Austin City Directory*, 225).

[46] Kate was Jane McCallum's sister, Kate Roy. Margaret was her daughter.

[47] Governor Hobby was Ferguson's opponent in the July 1918 Democratic gubernatorial primary, the first opportunity women had to go to the polls. In mid-April Travis County women organized a Hobby Club to assist in the campaign (*Handbook of Texas*, 1:591-92 and 3:396). Jane McCallum was a member of the advisory committee of the Austin Hobby Club, along with Elizabeth Eby, Nell Doom, Julia Goeth, and Carrie Hart (*Austin Statesman*, Apr. 17, 1918, p. 8). Eby, married to Dr. Frederick Eby, had succeeded Jane McCallum as president of the Austin Equal Suffrage Association in 1917. Though originally elected, Mrs. Haines apparently did not serve in this position.

[48] The first woman candidate for statewide office in Texas, Annie Webb Blanton de-

of Pub[lic] Instruction Doughty. The latter and wife both milk & water sops—wish could time record my conversation with her when she 'phoned to ask if I am going to support her husband.

The fool killer must be fighting the Kaiser—or I'd not be here to tell tale of how I raised $3,500^{00} at State Suf.[frage] meeting while so dead tired I just didn't mind being my silly crazy self before the crowd—and they came across.

Tonight I feel bereft—Alvaro and Arthur left for wheat fields last night, and Hubert, who is in line for his majority, left yesterday for France via New York. Alvaro gave up $60^{00} job to answer government's call for harvesters—and Arthur begged so to go we let him. Mary Lee left this morning for home—and I just realize[d] that her coming in & going out like Kathleen is forever past—she'll teach next year. Roger Harris has been visiting boys, but is with Pete Smith now. K[athleen] is spending night with Annie Lewis Preston[.] Brown at party. Mr. M at Dr Suttons and Henry & mama asleep. Last night and nearly every day & night for weeks the house has been *running over* with *boys boys*—Arthur graduated other day, Alvaro last Feb. & both being rushed for frats. Then High School boys etc. etc. How I miss them all! When I waked this A.M. at 5:45 to get M.[ary] L.[ee] off and the birds were singing so happily, I wondered *how they could*. Think I hear my hubby—hope he has some ice cream—*hot hot*

Sunday June 16, 1918

I thought I had eaten and had seen others eat things "whut tasted good;"—but I never had—until last night for supper. We had some *all white wheat* hot biscuit with butter!! How Mr. M. & Brown & Henry are alive to tell the tale is because of the limitations of the baking pan! Quite a while before Texas voluntarily went on a wheatless basis all of this family except Mama, Kathleen & Henry, took a wheatless pledge which we have religiously kept—during the entire time I had one white bread roll—thro accident. The food administrater now advises that we eat a certain amount.[49]

feated incumbent Walter F. Doughty in the race for state superintendent of public instruction. In 1916 she had been elected the first woman president of the Texas State Teachers Association. She also served on the board of regents at Denton State Normal School, now Texas Woman's University (*Handbook of Texas*, 3:87-88; *American Statesman*, Sept. 15, 1918, sect. 2, p. 4).

[49]The United States was delinquent in its commitment to supply wheat to its European allies. The voluntary conservation of wheat was an effort to alleviate the shortage, as was the labor that Alvaro and Arthur, Jr., performed in the fields (*Austin American*, Mar. 24, 1918, p. 4).

A week ago today, while we were at train seeing Hubert off—for last time—what was said to be the sixteenth troop train passed through. I don't believe I *ever really knew hate* before; but as I looked at those children—boys in late teens & early twenties—all vim, energy and enthusiasm that at last they were off—as I looked at them and thought and thought—the horrid monster of hate was born full-fledged in my heart, and I fear if the Kaiser or any of his h— born minions had been in my power, no torture could have been too excruciating for me to have devised.—This is awful—there is no hate in me for the worst of his victims—his own people and soldiers—but for *him* and his *six, smirking, conceited* self pleased, well fed & clothed sons, "the *safest family in all Europe*" and for their kind. I hope God will let me live long enough to be forgiven for what it seems now I shall always feel. The more the war rages—tho, the more I believe that it is probable that "Forgive your enemies" does not apply to these fiends—that they are really the "devil loosed"

The boys on the *troop trains* (the very term has a stronger connotative value than any I know) have been ordered against demonstrations, but bursts of song and gleeful laughter came from every car. They waved and threw kisses and asked a few questions as they rolled past. One had his face covered with lather—and grinned at us over his busy razor. Another had a big unpeeled Irish potato held up to his mouth. Just here and there was glimpsed a rather sad expression—might have thought others on greatest adventure of their boyish lives.

O O O

Oh my! letter from boys—Arthur lost suit case and clothes, and one at Alva, the other at Enid. OK. They don't seem quite clear on how it happened themselves

Brown coming across on Summer School prop. all right. Glad there are no more *moustache* boys attending for him to *shave*. That *Brown* is at once a joy and a torment. He is so chock full of badness, and so loveable he can't be managed. His Spanish teacher, Fannie Preston, says she cannot look at him and keep a straight face—that his eyes are like twin batteries. Then the rascal said "You ought to understand him Mrs. Mc C—for his eyes and expression are yours over!"

I wonder if I am *too sympathetic* with their badness.

I don't seem to be able *quite enough* to forget my own youthful frolics, and I fear Mr. Stockard thinks I'm the limit because it never occurred to me to stop their April 1st dressing up, and because I helped Brown & Douglas prepare for the girls' baby party they attended. Just as if *any* body couldn't have seen those big hands and boy shoes sticking out from their fluffy ruffles!

Believe I'd have drawn the line tho if I'd been here last Summer when Brown blacked up & dressed the part, so he could get in the midst of things at the Negro Holy Rollers. Alvaro, bless his heart, lingered on the outskirts of the affair to see that no harm came to his *bad brother!*

Juneteenth 1918

Tomorrow paper day, have been sick with cold; got breakfast; worked all morning in outskirts explaining registering & voting to those poor, poverty stricken women. Pretty good success. Been sewing all aft.[ernoon] on K's dress. How *am* I to get a magazine article off that I have been asked to write. Tomorrow *last day* and not a line. Hobby Club meeting in A.M. Conference with Mrs. C[unningham] *before*—then work for paper and I'm *so* hot and tired—tired.

Sat June 29, 1918

Attained my majority at last, thank you, registered to vote[, the] 6th of Travis Co. women[,] at about 7.45 on June 26th. We had a lot of fun.

I seem to be always getting up and going down. Made three speeches for Hobby and the rest in three consecutive days[:] 1st at Confederate Woman's Home where we had to outwit Miss Daffin, 2nd at Go Valle where the women are fine; 3rd about 30 miles at Mt. Gaynor 6 miles beyond Dripping Springs in a regular Ferguson den.[50] Before I commenced speaking there seemed to be a million people—guess there really were *hundreds*—woods[?] *full*, and they treated me beautifully—laughed at my jokes and applauded frequently, but never in my life did I see any one heckled and treated as Mr. Yeiser when he finished his hour & 40 minute talk. They claim we made hosts of converts—could write a dozen pages about it. *Some* experience[51]

Sat. July 7, 1918

Doing organizing, sending "Women in Politics" to paper nearly every day besides [my regular] Sunday dept. and speaking & 'phone 'phone

[50]Katie Daffan was superintendent of the Confederate Woman's Home, a state institution, located in Hyde Park. She had been literary editor of the *Houston Chronicle* for a number of years and by this time had published several books of fiction and non-fiction (*1918 Austin City Directory*, 53; *Dallas News*, May 23, 1951). Govalle is now a part of far east Austin. Dripping Springs is in the Hill Country, about twenty-two miles west of Austin.

[51]McCallum made numerous speeches in support of Hobby's candidacy: at the Daughters of Rebecca, the Men's Confederate Home, Hornsby's Bend, Oak Hill, and a number of Austin public schools (*American Statesman*, Aug. 11, 1918, pp. 1, 2).

'phone—company—oh Gee! Last Tuesday spoke at High S.[chool] at 4:30—to Confederate Veterans at 7; spent Wed. aft. at Court house where women registering. Thursday did paper work and lived in a cyclone until left to speak at school house beyond Del Valle at 8:oclock Got home not until 2:00 next morning and I had to break & refuse engagements until I've just this minute promised to go to Manor tonight.[52]

Tuesday July 9, 1918
Thank the good Lord that the last entry in this book means so much for good honest government. An S.O.S. call came from Miss Blanton for funds; Mrs A. Caswell Ellis & I went to San Antonio yesterday to see Col. Brackenridge[53] & he saw that we returned with a check from Miss Eleanor for a cool $1000[00]!!

Sat. —July 20, 1918 [54]
Just got last batch of ballots off to community meeting. As chairman, appointed sub-chairmen in each ward who, in turn, appointed neighborhood chairmen. This last group we call together and explain to them the ins and outs of voting and tell them *why* we have endorsed certain candidates and impress upon them that women must cast *no tainted ballots*. This group in turn will hold meetings in every neighborhood in Austin next Monday (one Tuesday) and pass the information on down. If Austin women do not vote right it will be because they don't care to know. Don't know that I'll have courage to start another diary & so much is left out that this is next to none. Wish [I] could give accounts of speaking trips etc. Mt. Gaynor 6 miles beyond Dripping Springs in a Ferguson den was the most exciting. Have made several dozen speeches & talks—go by special invitation to Kyle next Wednesday[55]
Austin women who have nearly broken down in this work are Mrs. Will Hart, Mrs. J. B. Gay, Mrs. Frederick Eby, Mrs. Dave Doom, & J. A. Jackson. Also Mesdames John Preston, T. H. Bowman[,] J.E Williamson, Goldman[,] Claybrook[,] Gilfillan[56] and scores of others I've lost 18 lbs,

---

[52]Del Valle is about six miles southeast of Austin, while Manor is northeast of the city, a distance of about seventeen miles.
[53]George Washington Brackenridge was the brother of San Antonio suffragist Eleanor. He began making his sizable fortune after the Civil War by selling cotton. In addition, he was a banker, publisher, trust company president, and University of Texas regent (*Handbook of Texas*, 1:202).
[54]McCallum erased her penciled handwriting on this page before making her diary entry in ink. With the exception of several isolated words, the material is unretrievable.
[55]Kyle, Texas, is located about twenty-four miles south of Austin.
[56]Mollie Bowman was a widow, while Sallie Williamson's husband was a railroad

and must—so my *grandchildren* will know what we are going thro—tell of one day. Under my *right* arm developed a rising the size of half a hen egg—I went on speaking & working but Thursday—paper day—it nearly drove me wild, but I *had* to go on. "Mr Rabbit bleeged to clim dat tree" so with that; suffering I wrote & wrote and 'phoned & 'phoned on this committee work until 8 o'clock when I telephoned physician next door to come lance it as it must be ready. He had no cocaine and hesitated, but I held to the bed, gritted my teeth and had it done—expected to get right up & to work again but was too weak until yesterday morning.

The *records* we've found—the fun[?] over *questionnaires*[:] *everybody for suffrage* and *prohibition* now, the candidates, letters and visits! The men just *glory* in our direct way and open way of doing things. They say that the day of the candidate with a shady record is certainly past. It never occurs to us to refuse to tell *who* we are for and *why*, and when we hear certain men are for Ferguson what is there to do but *ask* them? if they refuse to tell we put them down for him. It is *some* smoking out process. Every woman in town will be telephoned & urged to vote for our candidates July 27.

During all of this, the Thetas gave a party out here decorated with electric lights & Jap.[anese] lanterns & it was beautiful. Just punch served. Dr. Vinson, Pres. [of the] University [of Texas] brought Elizabeth[57] & was to take her home at 10:30; so my task was to be entertaining to him so he'd forget time's passage! He, Mr. M. & I sat on lawn & really had *most* interesting time until 11:15! He told of new ~~plan~~ effort of Nations to try to keep boys in school and of the suggestion he is going to make at conference in Washington—a dandy one. as watched boys & girls dancing I could but think of those others in trenches and mine own in wheat fields—toiling.

Let this last entry tell of our great happiness over the victory of Franco-American troops—God will that they may continue victorious. It is *great* to be an American of *French* descent.

In order to inform the new voters about the complicated ballot and proper procedures at polling places, Elizabeth Eby coordinated a series

conductor. Nellie Goldman was married to a grocer. Elva Claybrook, a former head of the Texas Women's Press Association, wrote the *Austin American* article "Women of Texas and the Ballot," which appeared on June 23, 1918. Rosalie Gilfillan's daughter Susan is mentioned in McCallum's "Friday" diary entry of October 1916 (*Directory of the City of Austin: 1909-10* [Galveston, 1909], 47; *1918 Austin City Directory*, 164, 189, 204, 236, 238, 443).

[57]Mary Elizabeth Vinson was the daughter of the university president (*Austin City Directory—1920* [Houston, 1920], 409).

of schools for voting, most of which were held in public school buildings.[58] Some of Jane McCallum's last minute advice to the women appeared in her columns in the *Austin Statesman* in the days just prior to the primary election. These items describe some of the electioneering tactics that might confuse women voting for the first time.

A recent report is to the effect that a "mere man" acted as advisor to a body of new voters and told them they "might write the election judge's name on the ballot["] themselves if it was not there. Unless the women have over 500 dollars lying around that they wish to be rid of they'd best let the election judge do his own writing.[59]

Do not believe current stories to the effect that your ballot will be thrown out if you vote for certain candidates. It is your privilege to vote for any candid[a]te whose name appears on your ballot. If it would be illegal to vote for him, his name will not be there.[60]

Some of what McCallum called "parting admonitions" were practical; some were partisan.

Go to the polls thrice armed with a black pencil, good humored patience and your registration receipt. . . .

Take no list of candidates with you and call no candidate's name after you are within 100 feet of the polls. . . .

Vote by marking out with your black pencil the names of all candidates except the ones you wish to vote for. Naturally you can vote for only one man for each office, so if you leave two names not marked for one office your vote is not counted for either. . . .

Do not let anyone see how you have voted. . . .[61]

William Pettus Hobby.

Remember, please, that if your first vote is not cast for the man who made it possible for you to have a vote you many never cast a second vote.[62]

[58]*Austin Statesman*, June 23, 1918, sect. 2, p. 2; *Austin Statesman*, June 30, 1918, p. 5.
[59]*Austin Statesman*, July 25, 1918, p. 4.
[60]*Austin Statesman*, July 26, 1918, p. 5.
[61]Ibid.
[62]Ibid.

Her composition book filled to the bottom of its back cardboard cover, Jane McCallum suspended diary writing from July until the last day of 1918. She kept up many of her other activities during the remainder of the year, however, in the belief that since women had finally voted, they could "reconsecrate" themselves "to constructive war-winning work."[63]

For McCallum, war work meant the Fourth Liberty Loan drive and jobs with the Red Cross. She boosted women's efforts on the home front through her "Woman and Her Ways" column, which she contributed weekly to the *Austin Statesman* through May 1919. The newspaper also provided a forum for promoting the candidacies of William P. Hobby for governor and Annie Webb Blanton for state superintendent of public instruction.

McCallum continued to serve on the executive board of the Texas Equal Suffrage Association (TESA). In the fall of 1918 the board reaffirmed its conviction that a state constitutional amendment for full woman suffrage should not be proposed until after the war.[64] TESA members could use their energy more effectively in working for the federal suffrage amendment which, they expected, would pass the U.S. Senate by January 1919 at the latest. The women could focus on lobbying state legislators. If they could win support from two-thirds of the members of each house, Texas's part in the ratification process would be complete.

In contrast to securing a federal amendment, the work required to amend the state constitution to give women full suffrage seemed an ordeal. Not only was the legislature's approval necessary, but so was the voters'. To win such a referendum, a forceful statewide campaign would be imperative. But this would drain TESA's already depleted treasury, the argument ran, and it would distract members from essential war work. Moreover, holding a plebiscite in the first part of the year would effectively disenfranchise all the servicemen who were abroad, a group that was counted on to express its appreciation for the women's work by supporting full suffrage. Although the armistice signed on November 11, 1918, had ended the fighting in Europe, demobilization was a slow process. Registration and poll tax deadlines might pass for all but the very first veterans to come home.

Consequently, at its November board meeting the TESA appointed

---

[63] *Austin Statesman*, July 28, 1918, sect. 2, p. 1.
[64] The narrative in this and the next four paragraphs is based on Nieuwenhuizen, "Minnie Fisher Cunningham and Jane Y. McCallum," 41-45.

a ratification committee, also referred to as the legislative committee, named Jane Y. McCallum as chairman, and prepared to lobby state legislators for the soon-to-be-passed federal amendment. Minnie Fisher Cunningham accepted a call to the headquarters of the National American Woman Suffrage Association in Washington, D.C., to lobby southern Democrats in the U.S. Senate.

Trouble soon began to brew. Several prominent women, including some TESA leaders, saw good reason to press for an early vote in the Texas legislature on the state suffrage amendment.[65] In addition to advocating woman suffrage, they were strong prohibitionists who believed that they needed women's votes to pass a prohibition amendment over the vigorous and well-financed liquor lobby. They expected the legislature to vote on prohibition during the 1919 session, but wanted suffrage to be enacted first. Since progressive prohibitionists now controlled the state Democratic party, this line of reasoning carried weight with the legislature.[66]

The women believed the argument had merit for suffragists as well. Suffragists could be sure of support from prohibitionists in an early referendum. However, if prohibition were to be voted on first and the suffrage amendment postponed, the drys would not be as enthusiastically behind the women.[67] Suffragists with strong sympathies toward the prohibition cause thus succeeded in dividing the TESA leadership over a question of strategy.

A problem of a different nature arose in the last weeks of 1918. Jesse Daniel Ames of Georgetown, TESA treasurer, had been more or less left to run the organization in Austin, along with Jane McCallum, during Cunningham's absence. Ames did not consider McCallum equal to the task. She begged Cunningham to return to Austin because McCallum lacked "self confidence" and a "state wide reputation." She was "not a leader in any sense," as she was "panicky already."[68] Whatever motivated this outpouring of ill will, Ames injected a per-

[65]Most notably, these Dallas women included Nannie Webb Curtis, president of the Texas Woman's Christian Temperance Union, Vernice Reppert, second vice president of TESA, and Marguerite Davis, TESA recording secretary and wife of state representative John Davis (Nieuwenhuizen, "Minnie Fisher Cunningham and Jane Y. McCallum," 43, 44; Moreland, *Texas Women*, 148-49).

[66]Gould, *Progressives and Prohibitionists*, 247, 254.

[67]Vernice Reppert to Minnie Fisher Cunningham, Dec. 13, 1918, quoted in Nieuwenhuizen, "Minnie Fisher Cunningham and Jane Y. McCallum," 45.

[68]Jessie Daniel Ames to Minnie Fisher Cunningham, Dec. 21, 1918, Series G, #164, McCP, I. Ames's unsatisfying childhood and disastrous marriage as well as her contributions during the 1920s and 1930s to the Committee on Interracial Cooperation and the Association of Southern Women for the Prevention of Lynching are recounted in her biog-

sonal element into the situation which was hardly conducive to harmonious relations and collaborative efforts.

Ames also joined other TESA members who were wavering on the question of early submission during the last days of 1918.[69] TESA could not sustain the position taken at its November 1918 board meeting. In the end, events forced the board to accept the fact that the state suffrage amendment would be submitted to the legislature, which was soon to convene. On January 15 the U.S. Senate agreed to delay its vote on the federal suffrage amendment, as proponents were one vote shy of passage. Then Governor Hobby, perhaps yielding to pressure from legislators and prohibitionists, called for consideration of the Texas amendment.[70]

Jane Y. McCallum issued a statement to the press on January 18 which conceded the inevitable. The *Austin Statesman* published it in full. The statement is a masterpiece of transforming factional infighting into rational discussion among friends. It also reveals that McCallum, for one, was not ready to concede an early date for the referendum.

Judging from the contents of numerous letters received at headquarters from friends in various parts of the State, an impression has gone out that would be serious were it not so manifestly absurd and unfounded. These friends have been informed that there is what one expresses as "a great row among the women leaders at the Capitol."

Letters have been sent stating the facts and asking for the source of this misinformation, but as such reports spread rapidly I have decided, as chairman of the legislative committee of the Texas Equal Suffrage Association, to issue a statement.

As always among intelligent people, there have been differences of opinion. In this particular instance the differences concerned chiefly the time our amendment should be submitted. There were a number of straightforward, candid, but perfectly friendly arguments on the subject, and I am happy to be able to make the positive assertion that if there has been any "fight" or even breaking of friendly relations between the

raphy by Jacquelyn Dowd Hall, *Revolt against Chivalry: Jessie Daniel Ames and the Women's Campaign Against Lynching* (New York, 1979). Hall attributes the grating between the two women to McCallum's perception of Ames as a rough hewn "country woman" and Ames's identification of McCallum as the epitome of a southern lady (p. 117).

[69]Jessie Daniel Ames to Minnie Fisher Cunningham, Dec. 28, 1918, Series G, #164, McCP, I.

[70]*Austin American*, Jan. 16, 1919, p. 1; *Austin American*, Jan. 17, 1919, p. 8.

women who are here earnestly seeking full enfranchisement for their sex,
I know nothing of the matter nor can I learn of anyone else who does.

The difference as to year was quickly and definitely settled when, on
the same morning, Governor Hobby in his message asked for submission
at the earliest possible date, and the United States Senate failed to pass the
Federal Amendment.

The difference as to the month continues to call for discussion. Some
feel that both suffrage and prohibition should be taken at their full tide
and voted upon in May, while others just as sincerely contend that the
time should be set in the summer after the women have had time to
recuperate from the Fifth Liberty Loan campaign and when the farmers
will be having more leisure to go to the poles. The discussions are
interesting and likely to continue, but Texas women are so confident that
the members of the Thirty-sixth legislature are their friends and are
giving equal suffrage the most earnest and intelligent consideration, that
they will gladly abide that body's decision.

The Texas Equal Suffrage Association already is thoroughly organized and merely awaits the settling of the date before launching an active
campaign in every county in the state.[71]

It was, in fact, less than a week following this statement that both
houses of the state legislature passed the suffrage amendment. They
set an early date of May 24 for referenda on four items, including
suffrage and prohibition, as Governor Hobby preferred.

In addition to the provision permitting women to vote, the suffrage
amendment included a citizenship clause proposing that the filing of
"first papers"—an application for citizenship—would no longer qualify an individual to vote in future elections. Full citizenship would be
required of every voter.[72] The suffragists and their allies unfortunately
failed to realize how great an impact this clause would have on the
outcome of the referendum.

McCallum was soon able to announce that Minnie Fisher Cunningham was returning to Texas to lead the campaign.[73] For her own part,
McCallum agreed to head the press and publicity committee.

[71]The version reproduced here is the original mimeographed press release, signed by
Jane Y. McCallum, [Jan. 18, 1919], McCallum Papers, Part II, Austin History Center, Austin
Public Library (hereafter cited as McCP, II). It differs slightly from what the *Austin States-
man* printed on Jan. 19, 1919, p. 5.

[72]*Austin Statesman*, Jan. 22, 1919, p. 10; *Austin Statesman*, Jan. 25, 1919, p. 2.

[73]JYM to Co-Worker, Jan. 23, 1919, McCP, II.

Although Jane McCallum was on the brink of one of the busiest and most hectic six-month periods of her life, the suffrage issue was only one of her concerns as she doggedly kept up her diary for 1919. Her newspaper blitz early in the year had to yield occasionally to her family. Diary entries for the last six months of the year document McCallum's closeness to her children and her interest in the 1920 gubernatorial primary.

The volume in which she wrote her notes for 1919 is a small maroon clothbound "Daily Reminder" book, with each date printed at the top of a separate page.[74] Once again, McCallum made use of a journal which originally had a different purpose. In her entry for October 30 she states that she had bought it for Alvaro when she expected him to be drafted.

The diary is written legibly, mainly in pencil, and, as with the earlier diary, there is evidence that McCallum reread it at a later date. In two instances the bottom of a page, including some handwriting, has been torn off. She inserted strips of paper at many entries, marked in her handwriting "Suffrage" or "Imp[ortant]." Paragraphing in this volume is extremely difficult to detect. Perhaps because of the small format of the pages, indentations are miniscule where they exist at all.

In comparison with the 1916-1918 diary, many of the entries in the 1919 record book seem less rich and more hastily written, as though there were, as McCallum noted, "No time for diaries."[75] The value of the document, however, lies in McCallum's first hand accounts of the suffrage campaigns and in what it adds to our picture of the author herself.

Dec 31st 1918

The last day of this memorable year, in addition to household duties, cooking two meals etc. met with joint committee of Daughters of Confederacy and *suffragists* and presented petition that the old veterans had turned over to me and which contained 135 of their signatures to Gov. Hobby asking for *women* on their [the veterans'] Board to look after them in their old age as they plaintively put it.[76] Went to *Suffrage* Hdqts and got

[74]The editor is very grateful to Betty Jane McCallum Ozbun for making this diary, along with other papers in her possession, available for transcription.

[75]See below, diary entry for Apr. 9, 1919.

[76]Governor Hobby had to turn the request down, since only voters could serve on these boards. He agreed, however, to recommend changing the law (*Austin American*, Jan. 2, 1919, p. 4).

out a lot of letters—one to each representative. Spent som[e] time at Statesman office. *Paid poll tax*[77] and with Mrs. Ellis made some investigations there at C[ourt]-House.

[Reminder book page for Jan. 5, 1919]

Henry Y.[elvington] over for day, especially to interview the Governor on his prison reform ideas which H.[enry] is championing in S.[an] A.[ntonio] Evening News. Promises of gov. all right. A day of good-byes again—there were so many of these last year that they were the rule rather than the exception. First Hubert, (Cap.[tain] Jones) left for hospital again after 60 days furlough. Then Douglas McGregor came to say "good-bye" as he leaves for school in Bingham, and then Henry left for S.A. The last time Hubert & Henry were here together, how different, both preparing to go to officer's training camp. Now Hubert probably injured for life.[78] Refused Henry because [the enlistment officers] said [he has] too

[continued on reminder book page for Jan. 6, 1919]
many children—of *course* he has & should not want to go![79]

Received a pile of mail—8 letters from Legislators in reply to mine on suffrage attitude. Made Arthur shirt out of 1 that didn't fit his dad. Old confederat[e] veteran came to ask me to aid him in getting to be assistant door keeper of Senate.

[Feb. 5, 1919]

A *memorable day* —
So sorry couldn't go down to capital for signing —[80]
(*Later:* wish I had stated *why* I couldn't go. Mamma or one of the children must have been ill)

JYM

[77]The poll tax had been waived for the 1918 primary. To participate in the March 1919 city primary, women had to present receipts as evidence that they had paid the $1.75 poll tax by February 1. Those over sixty years of age needed certificates of exemption by the same deadline (*Austin American,* Jan. 22, 1919, p. 4; *Austin Statesman,* Mar. 20, 1919, p. 10).

[78]Hubert Jones had gone to France with his outfit in October 1917 after completing his training at Leon Springs. He was promoted to the rank of captain and served on a general's staff. After his injury and a lengthy hospital stay he returned to Austin in November 1918. He was never able to walk normally after the injury (*Austin American,* Oct. 20, 1917, sect. 2, p. 2; *Austin Statesman,* Nov. 12, 1918, p. 6; Editor's interview with Mrs. A. N. McCallum, Jr., Nov. 20, 1986).

[79]Henry Yelvington had seven surviving children at his death in 1944 (*San Marcos Record,* Mar. 3, 1944, folder on Henry Yelvington, McCP, II).

[80]Governor Hobby signed the full suffrage resolution in the senate chamber on this date.

[Feb. 12, 1919]
Big suffrage luncheon at Driskill and State Board meeting & Ratification Com.[mittee] meeting.[81] Promised mamma and family to make this my last appearance for a *long time.*

[Feb. 22, 1919]
Next time I "retire" from public life [I] shant announce it as today have had to refuse—*now that I have time*—to accept city chairmanship again for Liberty Loan, State treasurership and Board member of Colonial Dames and to attend *Serbian* relief com. meeting where "especially desired."[82] This a lonesome hour as my hubby left for Chicago to attend Dep[artmen]t. of Sup[erintenden]t.[s] of N.[ational] E.[ducation] A.[ssociation] at 9.30 thi[s] A.M.

[bottom of page torn off [83]]

[Feb. 23, 1919]
interesting letters from Charlie and Carl.[84]—both still in France

[Feb. 28, 1919]
I am lonesome for my little girl tonight.[85] The Frosh dance comes off— *if* the Freshmen permit—and the s[ophomore] boys are at K.[nights of] C.[olumbus] Hall to do their share of preventing it.[86] But it all takes me back to *other* Frosh-Fresh dances when Kathleen was such an active

Minnie Fisher Cunningham was present, among others (*Austin Statesman,* Feb. 5, 1919, p. 3).

[81]The Austin Equal Suffrage Association hosted Mrs. Hobby and the wives of Texas legislators at their luncheon, which the *Statesman* extolled as "brilliant in the extreme." McCallum's toast, one of several on the program, was entitled "The Power Behind the Throne" (*Austin Statesman,* Feb. 13, 1919, p. 8).

[82]Serbia (now a part of Yugoslavia) had been overrun during World War I. Although unable to aid in the relief effort for these victims of the war, McCallum was named to a Czecho-Slovak Relief Committee in June. This group raised funds for food and clothing (*Austin American,* June 18, 1919, p. 2).

[83]Given the care with which the page was torn and the nature of the material which follows on the reverse page, it appears that part of the entry was deliberately excised.

[84]These young men are doubtless Kathleen's friends, Charlie Freeman and Carl Squier. (For Squier, see the diary entries for Dec. 8, 1917, and Jan. 21, 1918.)

[85]Kathleen was teaching school in Pearsall, Texas, a town about fifty miles southwest of San Antonio. See the entry for Apr. 5, 1919.

[86]It was traditional at the University of Texas for sophomore men to try to prevent or delay the start of this dance. In 1919 the freshmen secretly changed the location of the event from the Driskill to the Elks Club. "A half-hearted egg fight . . . gave a suggestion of the spirit of other days, but the Sophs were outnumbered and outgeneraled" (*1919 Cactus* [n.p., n.d.], 376).

interested participant and I miss her—and dressing her—and the flurry and girlish part of it all. Bless the old boys—they certainly arent letting studies interfere greatly with [t]heir college careers [page torn] [th]is exciting week.

[Mar. 10, 1919]

Commenced going to Suffrage Headquarters every day to do publicity work. *May be* my rest *will* come after May 24, but no time for slackers now.

[Mar. 11, 1919]

Mrs. Cunningham (Minnie) received word of death of her only brother in France. As if she didn't have more than she can bear now!

Leaves for her mother tonight

[Mar. 12, 1919]

Mr. McCallum and Hubert come to Headqtrs to see me *after* they've eaten lunch, so make them take me for some. Mr. M. takes H. on to osteopath. Hard day.

[Mar. 13, 1919]

sick

Boys[,] mama & Mr. M. all wait on me.

[Mar. 14, 1919]

Sick, but manage to get out Statesman work.

(Captain) & Lester Brenizer, Hubert & Mary Helen [Holden?] here in aft.[ernoon]

Boys concerned over exams.

[Mar. 15, 1919]

Most interesting talk with ex-Gov. Sayers. *He* gave me a suffrage interview, and we talked of suffrage, prohibition, reconstruction problems, people who ride in automobiles and don't pay their grocery bills, the "human nature" one sees on street cars, border conditions[,] the citizenship clause in our bill etc.

[Mar. 16, 1919]

Sayers interv[i]ew *came out* in *big dailies* O.K.[87]

[87]In expressing his strong support for the state constitutional amendment, former

Rev. & Mrs. Read spent day on way to Arizona for a months vacation for his health. Mrs. R. discouraged over Huberts slow improvement on Mary Lee's account—sad, sad.

Guests in evening and as have no cook yet was pretty worn out

[Mar. 17, 1919]

This morning was almost too much for me, but went to Campaign (Suffrage) Headquarters and did what I could. Feel *so* sorry for Minnie. Mrs. Doom and I got *advice* from Senators Dorrough, Witt & Hertzberg in morning!

Also saw Adrian Poole over situation in his district which he promises to work hard on[88]

[Mar. 25 and 26, 1919]

All during these days [I have been] going to State Suffrage Headquarters daily and getting out stories etc. Being an amateur [I] was naturally proud to have Speaker Thomason, compliment highly [the] interview I wrote for him.[89] Papers all over State gave it good place[.] Glad my press stories are all accepted as if I were a veteran.

[Apr. 3, 1919]

State Suffrage School opened at Driskill[90]

[Apr. 5, 1919]

Went to Pearsall in reply to a homesick letter to see my precious little girl. Never in my wildest dreams did I picture a country so beautiful with wild flowers as between S.[an] A.[ntonio] and Pearsall is. Poppies, poppies every where and every color of red from deepest to lightest pink,

Governor Joseph D. Sayers defended women's right to vote as well as "to take an active and substantial part in the administration of public affairs" (*Dallas Morning News*, Mar. 16, 1919, p. 3, and *San Antonio Express*, Mar. 16, 1919, p. 5).

[88]R. P. Dorough represented Texarkana, and Harry Hertzberg was from San Antonio. Edgar Witt of Waco later served two terms as lieutenant governor. State Representative Adrian Pool was from El Paso (*Members of the Texas Legislature*, 265, 266, 269; *Handbook of Texas*, 3:1123).

[89]As the interview appeared in an Austin paper, R. E. Thomason of El Paso strongly endorsed the suffrage resolution and emphasized the importance of the citizenship (or alien) clause (*Austin Statesman*, Mar. 20, 1919, p. 6). (See the diary entry for July 3 and 4, 1919, and n137, below.)

[90]During the three days of suffrage school sessions the conferees heard speeches on election law, campaign publicity, public speaking, finance, and organization from experts including Mrs. A. O. Hughston of the National American Woman Suffrage Association, Judge W. M. Key of the Court of Civil Appeals, Dudley Woodward, Roy Bedichek, and A. Caswell Ellis (*Austin Statesman*, Mar. 30, 1919, p. 10, and Apr. 4, 1919, p. 10).

these all mixed in with white ones. Every other kind of Texas flower and the huisache chapparel (?) and *everything* in bloom. K.[athleen] & Zatella met me at train and I most cried, with joy over my child

[Apr. 8, 1919]
After 2 wild chases for train[, I] left Pearsall at 4.30 instead of 2

[Apr. 9, 1919]
Whew—but the work that accumulated while I was away. No time for diaries
Got a cook but dont fancy her.

[Apr. 11, 1919]
Mamma left to visit Jesse at Smithville[91]

[Apr. 12, 1919]
Worked all day as usual at Headquarters.
Went to House of Representatives to hear famous Dr. *Anna Howard Shaw* on Suffrage.
House and galleries crowded (estimated 2000 by papers), and she was simply splended![92] No one would ever dream that she is 72 years old.

I Dr. Anna Howard Shaw
[Apr. 13, 1919]
Just as [I] started to dress for church Mrs. Ellis telephoned for me to go for drive with her, Dr. Ellis, Mrs Pearce[,] Mrs. Cunningham and Dr. *Shaw*.
They gave me the seat next [to] the noted visitor and I found her as human, humorous and delightful a conversationalist as speaker. The drive on the Bee Cave road was wonderful.
Dr. Shaw says people should never know how old they are [and] that she doesn't *feel* one day older than she did twenty years ago except when she realizes her years[93]

[91]Jesse Yelvington was apparently ministering to a congregation in Smithville, about forty miles southwest of Austin.
[92]Anna Howard Shaw, M.D., presided over the National American Woman Suffrage Association from 1904 to 1915. She was considered a better orator than administrator. Both Jane McCallum and her husband sat on the platform for this occasion. Shaw's lively address ranged over topics such as the loyalty of southern women to their country, women's war work, the role women could play in peace negotiations, and the injustice of denying soldiers their votes (Fowler, *Carrie Catt*, 25-26; *Austin Statesman*, Apr. 14, 1919, p. 2).
[93]Ironically, Shaw died on July 2, 1919 (*Who Was Who in America, Vol. I: 1897-1942* [Chicago, 1943], 1110).

[Apr. 14, 1919]

Work, work, work[.] Press *stories, interviews*[,] *bulletins* etc.

Had to fire cook.

Alvaro McCallum is the very salt of the earth. How I do thank God for such a son

[Sunday, Apr. 20, 1919]

After cooking breakfast every morning, working *my brain* all day, then my hands again when [I] get home from office at night, Sunday is indeed a welcome day.

[Apr. 25, 1919]

Mamma came home and I was *some* glad to see her.

[Apr. 29, 1919]

Hear so many nice things about my State publicity work, but I can only look upon it with an "ironic indulgence." Mrs. Cunningham declares it is superb.

Seems funny that the big dailies print everything I send them.

McCallum's humility notwithstanding, the press and publicity work was well organized and effective. Largely as a result of her efforts, volumes of letters, press releases, and bulletins deluged the offices of newspaper editors throughout the state, as well as the desks of four hundred people designated as campaign chairmen for senatorial districts, cities, and counties. Just prior to the referendum, Minnie Fisher Cunningham claimed that "more than ninety small papers have issued a four page equal suffrage supplement. Countless editorials and many columns of news-matter concerning the progress of the campaign have been given space; in fact, the past week we have found it impossible to read half of our clippings."[94]

McCallum eased her writing burden by calling on others to supply the raw material, as shown in this excerpt from a letter to county chairmen detailing her plans for a weekly suffrage newspaper.

In order to have a paper that is really worth while—one representative and effective—all portions of the state should have a part in it; and this is to ask you to immediately select some capable, enthusiastic, honest-to-

---

[94] "For Release Friday May 23rd," typescript, p. 2, Series A.3, McCP, I.

goodness suffragist who is gifted with what in newspaper parlance is termed a "nose for news" and have her send to Headquarters once, or several times a week, little spicy bits of Suffrage news; short accounts of meetings; expressions from well known residents and any other matter that she feels will make interesting reading for the people of the State.[95]

McCallum also solicited testimonials from her acquaintances and from Texas political and social leaders, though she barely had the time to acknowledge them. McCallum belatedly thanked Anna Pennybacker for an endorsement she had sent.

[I] am not even saying "excuse me" for not writing before, because I know that *you* know when I have to choose between letters to friends and enemies the last must come first . . . ![96]

McCallum also kept track of suffrage quips that were making the rounds. Although these examples are probably not products of her considerable wit, she recorded them in her own hand.

Suffrage knockers are put here for a purpose—same as "flu" germs and first days of the month

Suffragist: "If a party participated in by men only is a 'stag party,' is not a nation whose government is participated in by men only 'stag-nation'?"

Mere Man: "But a nation participated in by women only would be dam(e)nation"

Suffragist: "Then our duty is clear—we'll have a combi-nation."

The Texas young man acquired suffrage just as he acquired his moustache, by the simple expedient of growing older; the immigrant man acquired suffrage by living here long enough to "declare his intentions" of some day becoming a citizen; but the Texas woman acquired suffrage by fighting every inch of the way.[97]

[95]JYM to County Chairman, Mar. 10, 1919, Series A, McCP, I.

[96]JYM to Mrs. Percy V. Pennybacker, May 1, 1919, Series A, McCP, I.

[97]Ms page of quips, on reverse of copy of press release of Apr. 22, 1919, Series A.3, McCP, I; Ms page, Series A.3, McCP, I.

Amidst the mounting flurry of press activity, McCallum found herself facing a special legislative session called to consider a bill which would allow returned soldiers to vote in the referendum on May 24 without having paid the poll tax. In March Governor Hobby had vetoed a similar bill, which his attorney general had deemed unconstitutional.[98] Since that time, three state district judges had ruled otherwise, and prospects for the bill's passage were encouraging.[99]

[May 5, 1919]
Legislature called together to arrange for soldiers to vote. Mrs. Cunningham[,] Mrs. Doom and I *started them off!!* We all lunched together at Driskill and I got *beau camp*[100] interviews from leaders for my press stories.

[Tuesday, May 6, 1919]
Lonnie McKean and Harris Brush (captain) came to office on my invitation to talk over [the] soldier voting problem. Earlier I had gone to see Dr's Beverly and Loving. Lonnie[, who was] responsible for [the] petition[,] & others didn't realize the "swat 'em all" clause was in it.[101]

Wed. A.M. went up to Mrs. Rudolphs (8th floor) to see about multographing & ran into Mr. Kerby & prohibition Hdqts.[102] Theirs cant touch our organization. Mr. K. voluntarily gave me $50.00 (check to Mrs Ellis) for *local suffrage.*

[Wednesday, May 7, 1919]
Such a pleasant surprise this afternoon. A fine looking young officer (Lieut) was ushered into my office and so glad to see me and for the *life* of me I couldnt place him. Turned out to be *Verne Taylor* who[,] 8 years

[98]*Austin Statesman*, Mar. 19, 1919, p. 1.
[99]*Austin Statesman*, May 4, 1919, sect. 2, p. 4.
[100]McCallum meant "beaucoup," French for "many."
[101]Lawyer Alonzo T. McKean was circulating a petition to the state legislature to postpone the referenda on woman suffrage and prohibition until the fall, by which time most Texas servicemen would have returned. Among the ex-soldiers who signed the petition was Dr. A. F. Beverly. The "swat 'em all clause" may refer to the wording in the document which called on sympathizers to vote against all of the proposed constitutional amendments if the legislature failed to postpone the referenda (*Austin American*, May 5, 1919, pp. 1, 3). Jane McCallum viewed these tactics as self-defeating.
[102]R. Harper Kirby was chairman of the State Prohibition Committee (*Austin American*, May 24, 1919, p. 2).

ago when he was only 18[,] used to confide his love affairs to me. He has been in Idaho while not in service and is [a] very promising lawyer. We spent 2 hours talking over old times & his old girls.

Allen Wight—now Captain [—] blew in the office to see me last week. Told so many interesting stories of his life in France & on firing line.

[May 8, 1919]

Mercy on me, but I'm one tired mortal. Got out long *press* story for Sat[.]—wrote one for Sun[.], got out bulletin of 4 pages for Mother's Day (*soldier's* letters) and my weekly letter to chairmen.

Lonnie McKean came in again. He hasn't a thimblefull of sense but barrels of egotism.—Oh, gracious these know it alls!

The soldiers' letters referred to here were an ingenious ploy to gain publicity thirteen days before the referendum. On May 9 Governor Hobby signed the bill exempting returned soldiers from paying the poll tax, thus adding to the significance of their votes.[103] McCallum had enthusiastically outlined her idea to the county chairmen several weeks earlier.

The time has arrived for us to bring our cause home to the voters of Texas through the weekly and semi-weekly press as never before. The anti[-suffrage] forces are very small compared to the suffrage forces, but they are thoroughly organized and not missing an opportunity or losing a minute. They seem to have an unlimited supply of money to use in seeing that democracy does not prevail in Texas. It is our task to see that it does, and this is to ask your earnest, hearty and immediate co-operation in putting over what I believe will be a very effective bit of publicity on Mother's Day, (May 12).[104] The plan is to have every paper in Texas, or at least one or more papers in every county in Texas to publish one or more letters on Mother's Day (or the nearest day thereto that the paper is issued) from returned soldiers who believe that their mothers, wives and sisters should have a voice in making the laws which govern them.

To make certain that the letter will be in the hands of the newspapers two or three days before time for publication, you or your publicity chairman should get in touch with the boys of your county AT ONCE.

[103]*Austin American*, May 10, 1919, p. 4.
[104]The Sunday which was Mother's Day was, in fact, May 11.

Ask that their letters tell of their appreciation of women's work, both at home and abroad, during the war, and of their desire to see the women of Texas fully enfranchised. You will probably find a number of boys who will prefer to talk to you of their views and have you write them. Strong, concise letters not too long will be the most effective; and now let's all pull together and flood the Texas press with expressions from the men who fought for democracy, but who find that they cannot vote for it.[105]

As the date for the vote drew closer, McCallum's missives to county chairmen increased in frequency. She made suggestions, prodded, pumped up, and even tried to frighten her colleagues.

[The antis] are working secretly, but so effectively that every person calling himself a man in the State of Texas who is opposed to equal suffrage will be at the polls, rain or shine. Therefore, -rain, shine, hail or storm; sick, well, lunch or no lunch, I know that you will see that each honest-to-goodness red-blooded loyal American man entitled to vote will be there also.[106]

Excellent publicity can be obtained by having trades, business, farming and professional men write suffrage letters to the editor. Another corking plan is to ask merchants to devote their advertising space in local papers to our cause a number of times between now and May 24.

Will you not have these things done? The probability of having the soldier's vote should put new life into us all, and let us never forget that May 24 is 24 hours nearer every day!

DO send me an occasional letter, note, clipping or SOMETHING to indicate that my letters and bulletins aren't all being thrown into a bottomless abyss![107]

McCallum's labors put her in high spirits during May, although the blank diary pages are evidence that she had time to write only for the press and publicity committee. She voiced her optimism about the outcome of the vote in a letter to an officer of the National American Woman Suffrage Association, publishers of the *Woman Citizen*.

[105]JYM to County Chairman, Apr. 22, 1919, Series A.3, McCP, I.
[106]JYM to Co-Worker, May 20, 1919, Series A.3, McCP, I.
[107]JYM to County Chairman, May 1, 1919, Series A.3, McCP, I.

I feel that I have been most derelict in my duty in not keeping the Woman Citizen posted on the Texas campaign, but in our effort to arouse a State press consisting of some eight or ten thousand newspapers you can easily see where we had very little time for talk about what we were doing.

Now clippings are being received in such quantities that we are undecided whether to rent an additional room for their accomodation or to begin having them carted and piled in readiness for the May 24th victory bon fire!

Seriously, Mrs. Cunningham has put over a remarkable campaign that is exciting the profound admiration[,] and I fear, a bit of the envy of the men of the wholly masculine conducted campaigns for the other three May 24th amendments. She has labored at such a terrific rate and under so great a strain however, that I fear for her after all is over.

If the weather is good, and brewery interests have not gotten in some very subtle, underhanded work we feel sure of victory May 24th.[108]

[May 24, 1919]

Sad day for Texas women, but just what we expected with so many of the State's best disfranchised by being in France, and all the Mexicans, Negroes, Republicans[,] I.W.Ws, Reds, socialists and "what-nots" including "first paper" Huns allowed to vote while loyal American women were not.

It was sad indeed. One woman felt "exactly as though there had been a death in the family."[109] McCallum must have written this entry several days after May 24, since the early results of the referendum had the suffrage amendment ahead. It passed in the city of Austin, but not by a margin great enough to carry Travis County. Statewide totals showed a deficit of some 25,000 votes.[110]

A number of factors contributed to these dispiriting results. Opponents of woman suffrage were well-financed and at least as professionally organized as the suffragists. Fraudulent ballots cost untold votes in twenty-eight counties. The suffragists had campaigned for a "yes" vote on the second item. But the order of items had been altered on the

[108]JYM to Miss Rose Young, May 17, 1919, Series A, McCP, I.
[109]Mary Heard Ellis to Jessie Daniel Ames, Saturday [June? 1919], folder of 1919 TESA correspondance, McCP, II.
[110]*Austin American*, May 25, 1919, p. 1; Nieuwenhuizen, "Minnie Fisher Cunningham and Jane Y. McCallum," 71.

irregular ballots. Minnie Fisher Cunningham also attributed the loss to the shortage of time and money and to overconfidence on the part of the workers.[111]

One obvious ingredient in the amendment's defeat, which McCallum points to in her May 24 entry, is that no "first paper" alien would have voted in favor of his disenfranchisement. The clause making full citizenship a qualification for voting guaranteed opposition from this group.

Fortunately for Jane McCallum, there was little time for moping. Not only were her sons' graduations imminent at the end of the school year, but on June 4 the long delayed federal constitutional amendment passed the U.S. Senate. Woman suffrage was now an issue solely for state legislatures to consider. Austin suffrage workers, with McCallum at the helm, girded themselves for their only remaining task: to persuade Texas legislators to ratify the Susan B. Anthony amendment.

[June 5, 1919]
9.50 P.M.

Just home from seeing my baby boy graduate from Wooldridge [Elementary School]. His daddy couldn't be there but Mamma and I went and Kathleen and Mary Lee took their "dates," Hubert and Allen Wight (Cap) along to see it well done.

Found telegram here to K from Charles [Freeman] saying
[3 vertical pencil lines]

[The next two entries for June 9 and 10 were mistakenly written on the pages for May.]

Meant for *June*
[May 9, 1919]

Went to High School to see *Brown* graduate this morning. Despite his 6 feet he was "class baby" in years (15)

He is one popular kid. Dinner parties and dances every single night.

Meant for *June*
[May 10, 1919]
June [written over "May"]
3 o'clock P.M.

Such an excitement!! Boys [are] all through with exams and on [a] tear

[111]Nieuwenhuizen, "Minnie Fisher Cunningham and Jane Y. McCallum," 71-72; Gould, *Progressives and Prohibitionists*, 255-56.

so [I] have been directing their surplus energy! Brought up the S.[chool of] M.[ilitary] A.[eronautics] lockers, mowed lawns and now the bees are *swarming* and such a time with their bells & pans etc. Charlie [Freeman] just arrived in his car from Dallas and Hubert just phoned M.[ary] L.[ee] R.[ead] he'd be out so girls buzzing around too[.] Varsity Circus parade at 4 and circus tonight. So happy over A getting straight with courses.[112]

[June 13, 1919]
Arthur left for wheat fields—what heart-aches when they go.

[June 14, 1919]
News came that Judge Glass died suddenly in Texarkanna last night[113]

[June 17, 1919]
Mary Lee left for home after visiting K[athleen] since May 23rd.
Went to Headquarters Mrs C[unningham] and I saw Judge Keeling,[114] who says ratefying Fed.[eral] amendment [is a] question of whether Legislature will obey instructions of democratic conventions *for* suffrage or Republicans[,] socialists[,] Germans & Negroes who participated in referendum. Says if latter better not have a democratic party at all. Lieut Gov. Johnson[115] stopped us to give encouragement. Went to see Mrs. Glass—poor little woman.
Charles down stair's[;] Mr. M studying

McCallum refers in the above entry to the dispute over bringing the issue of ratification of the Susan B. Anthony amendment before the legislative session called for June 23. It had not been specified in Governor Hobby's original call,[116] and the "anti" forces were uniting under the leadership of former Congressman Robert Henry. He claimed that the majority of Texas voters had recently rejected woman

[112]Both Alvaro and Arthur were students at the University of Texas at the time (Editor's interview with Betty Jane McCallum Ozbun, Dec. 1, 1986; Certificate of Status issued Oct. 31, 1986, to editor by the Registrar of the University of Texas at Austin).
[113]Judge Hiram Glass, an Austin resident, represented Texas railroads before the Texas Railroad Commission (*Austin American*, June 15, 1919, p. 2).
[114]Walter A. Keeling was a first assistant in the Attorney General's office (*1920 Austin City Directory*, 264).
[115]Former state Senator W. A. Johnson of Hall County was elected lieutenant governor in 1918 (*Handbook of Texas*, 1:917).
[116]Hobby convened the legislature to make state appropriations and to "act upon such other matters as may be presented by the governor" (*Austin Statesman*, June 13, 1919, p. 1).

suffrage at the polls and that their will was a mandate to the legislature. Moreover, he argued, to ratify the federal suffrage amendment would compromise a right reserved for the states and defended in the Civil War.[117]

The suffragists countered that voters in the May 24 referendum had rejected only the citizenship clause, not woman suffrage. Counties "dominated by foreigners" had furnished the crucial margin of defeat. Suffragists pointed out, in addition, that the state Democratic party platform, adopted in September 1918, committed party members to the federal amendment.[118]

McCallum's diary entries for the week beginning June 21 make fascinating reading. They constitute a subjective chronicle of events in the legislature during these critical days, accompanied by McCallum's candid impressions. Yet, the wealth of tantalizing detail may bewilder the reader who lacks a grasp of the twists and turns of the legislative jousting.

The main lines of the story can be pieced together from contemporary newspaper accounts, although they omit any mention of Jane McCallum's activities. As legislators gathered in Austin for the special session, so too, did those who wished to influence them. On one side were Charlotte Rowe of the Women's National Anti-Suffrage Association and Pauline Wells, president of its Texas chapter[119] while McCallum reports the presence of proponents from the Texas Equal Suffrage Association (TESA), Mesdames Lindsey, Reppert, and Mahoney.

Those on each side of the ratification issue lobbied, made pronouncements, wrote letters, and held strategy meetings. At the start of the session, seventy-five House members signed a resolution proposing ratification, and Representative John Davis of Dallas, whose wife was recording secretary of TESA, reported 106 pledges of support from his colleagues. A similar resolution in the Senate had fifteen signatures. Senator Ed Westbrook of Hunt County agreed to manage the resolution on the floor.[120]

The first day's sessions were brief ones for both chambers. Governor Hobby sent his first message, placing the Susan B. Anthony

[117]*Austin Statesman*, June 16, 1919, p. 4.
[118]*Austin American*, June 22, 1919, p. 19.
[119]*Austin Statesman*, June 20, 1919, p. 3. Pauline Wells was married to Brownsville lawyer and Cameron County political boss James B. Wells for whom Jim Wells county was named. He was a central figure in south Texas politics as early as the 1880s and continued to wield power until about 1920 (*Handbook of Texas*, 2:878; Evan Anders, *Boss Rule in South Texas: The Progressive Era* [Austin, 1982], ix, 6).
[120]*Austin Statesman*, June 23, 1919, p. 1.

amendment on the agenda.[121] The resolutions for ratification could then be read to both groups. In the House the item was referred to the Committee on Constitutional Amendments, which, within hours and by a unanimous vote, recommended approval. Since several absent representatives wanted to vote on the measure, it was made the special order of business for 11:00 A.M. the following day. The Senate referred the resolution to committee after electing Paul D. Page, a supporter of woman suffrage from Bastrop, as president pro tem.[122]

June 24, as McCallum's diary attests, was the first of several days of parliamentary and rhetorical wrangling. In the House substitute motions, motions to table, and impassioned speeches complete with Biblical references, preceded the vote.[123] Speaker R. E. Thomason again earned McCallum's praise for shepherding the deliberations to a triumphant conclusion for the suffragists.

The Senate upheld its reputation as a fun house during its tussle over ratification. The *Austin American* agreed with McCallum's appraisal that the evening hearing of the Senate Committee on Constitutional Amendments "developed some laughable tilts . . . with the honors mainly on the side of the proponents."[124] Charlotte Rowe called woman suffrage "a menace to the future of the race." Pauline Wells testified that some of her friends who favored giving women the vote had stopped speaking to her. Senator J. C. McNealus, who had worked so diligently to win the vote for returning soldiers in the May 24 referendum and had previously supported woman suffrage, now was adamantly opposed. Minnie Fisher Cunningham "spoke briefly." At the conclusion of the hearing, the committee voted unanimously to recommend approval of Westbrook's resolution.[125]

Senate discussion of the measure slowed to a crawl in the next two days. McCallum noted that the recess for speeches by Arkansas Governor C. H. Brough and Judge William F. Ramsey (formerly of the Court of Criminal Appeals, at the time chairman of the Eleventh Federal Reserve District) on June 25 left her hanging in suspense. According to one newspaper report, the following day was largely wasted in considering alternative propositions, which for the most part were variations on the theme of postponing action. It was clear from the votes on these substitute propositions that the suffragists had

[121]*Austin American,* June 24, 1919, p. 1.
[122]*Austin American,* June 24, 1919, p. 1; *Austin Statesman,* June 23, 1919, p. 1.
[123]*Austin American,* June 25, 1919, pp. 1, 2; *Austin Statesman,* June 24, 1919, p. 1.
[124]*Austin American,* June 25, 1919, p. 2.
[125]*Austin Statesman,* June 25, 1919, p. 3.

a majority of the Senate behind them. Since so many eager voices wanted to be heard, however, the upper house adjourned for the day without voting on ratification.[126]

Senators concluded their arguments on Friday, June 27. R. M. Johnston of Harris County, a leader among the anti's on the Senate floor, summed up for those opposed. Senator Page spoke last for those in favor: "The man who votes against suffrage here and now may as well bow his head forever so far as political ambition is concerned, for women are going to vote in Texas and the women voters will remember who have been their friends." The original fifteen signers of the ratification resolution were joined by three new allies, giving the pro-suffrage forces a majority, and the victory was at last theirs.[127]

There remained for Saturday, June 28, only the final, or third reading of the resolution, which passed *viva voce*. The *Austin American* paid high tribute to the ever-present witnesses.

"[N]ot a few of the opponents of the resolution had gone to their homes.

But the Texas women who have watched the battle—and have taken no small part in it—were still in the galleries and they knew every stage of the proceeding that was taking Texas into suffrage ranks."[128]

[June 21, 1919]

Worked with members of Legislature all week—got out several press stories and open letter from Minnie to Senator McNealus. Took dinner at Driskill with her and Mary Ellis.[129] Dramatic performance by McNealus. Saw Senator Dudley—all well[.] Mr. Warner came down [and] wired for us to stop open letter.

[June 22, 1919]

Sick (usual) but had several phone conversations with Senator Westbrook about pairing. Sen. Witt who can't be here tomorrow. O.K. News of killing of Sen. Bell who was one of our signers.[130]

[126]*Austin American*, June 26, 1919, p. 3; *Austin American*, June 27, 1919, p. 3.

[127]*Austin American*, June 28, 1919, p. 4.

[128]*Austin American*, June 29, 1919, p. 1.

[129]Mary Ellis served as president of the Austin Equal Suffrage Association for 1918-19 (*1920 Austin City Directory*, 193; *Austin Statesman*, May 26, 1919, p. 4). See also Part 2, n26.

[130]Senator Edgar E. Witt remained paired for in the vote on June 27 (*Austin American*, June 28, 1919, p. 4). Senator W. S. Bell of Foard County was shot to death by members of his daughter-in-law's family (*Austin Statesman*, June 23, 1919, p. 5).

[June 23, 1919]

Legislature convened—at capitol at 9 o clock[.] Greatest joke: while Anti's were caucussing at Driskill about how to obtain [a] hearing before House Com.[mittee] our side brought up question[,] referred it to Com. & they reported it back unanimously recommending its passage—all before 12 o clock!! *Hardest task* [was] managing untrained enthusiasts, Mrs. Lindsey of Houston and the Dallas crowd Mrs Reppert & Mahoney, and keeping John Davis straight—biggest bone head out of scrap heap. Our bill [is a] special order at 11 tomorrow.

[June 24, 1919]

A day of wonderful experiences. Went with Minnie (Mrs. Cunningham[)] before Senate Committee at 9 o'clock. Hearing postponed until 4 P.M. (Anti's so queer looking) Lobbied. Went to House at 11, bill brought up promptly. Thomason great; test vote greatly in our favor. Plan to let Anti's do talking as we have votes. They raved (with only 1 talk from our side) until previous question ordered—at 3.55 [P.M.] speaker announced 20 against[,] 96 for!!! We rushed over to Senate hearing and *never* [had] so much fun. Miss Rowe from New York (Anti paid worker of breweries) raved. Cong. *Henry* & *Sen.* McNealus *both* anti's nearly fought over Jim Ferguson etc[.] Mrs. Wells scolded and we *smiled* & *smiled*. So proud of Minnie.

[June 25 and 26, 1919]

How we lived through these two days of fillibustering by the enemy is beyond me. The opposition tried every ~~way~~ conceivable method, honest & otherwise[,] to defer[,] delay or defeat. They had the notorious Quintins[?] Watson, Will Hanger[131] and Bob Henry (ex-U.S. Congressman) here to assist them, and Bagby (Lion of Lavaca) was openly coaching our senator Walter Caldwell,[132] but our men (God bless them) stood like a stone wall manned with gatling guns which they discharged most effectively at proper intervals. Senators Westbrook, Paul Page, Harry Hertzberg and Dudley of El Paso (not to mention Lieut. Gov. Johnson[;] not to mention 11 more who stood with us from first) *re-vived*

[131]Q. U. Watson of Giddings in Lee County served in the state Senate from 1907 to 1914 (*Members of the Texas Legislature*, 208, 217, 227, 236). William A. Hanger of Tarrant County was elected to the state Senate in 1898. When he retired after eight years, he resumed private law practice (H. T. Warner, Hugh Nugent Fitzgerald, et al., eds., *Texans and Their State: A Newspaper Reference Work* [Houston, n.d.], 71).

[132]One proposal to postpone action was ruled out of order by the chair. Travis County Senator Walter Caldwell appealed the ruling, which was subsequently sustained by a vote (*Austin American*, June 27, 1919, p. 3).

our pride in our *Texas men* as we watched them battle, attack, "bleed and die" for our cause. It was great, but recessed to listen to the Gov. of Arkansas & to Judge Ramsey orate before our fate was decided were awful. Many things will never be known. Mrs. Spell's warning to Governor of coming *delegation—his flight* to country club etc.

[June 27, 1919]

"Oh joy, oh boy," on a test vote we won. Alderdice, Woods etc.[133] finally going with us after fighting sufficiently to satisfy constituents opposed.

The bill thus passed to third reading which will be merely a matter of form for tomorrow morning.

[June 28, 1919]

Its all over—I can not realize that this thing we've been waging such a *terrific fight* for is now actually a matter of *history.* Somehow [I] felt too thankful to be jubilant: we've a great responsibility and I pray God we may meet it squarely and successfully.

The last act of the enemy was to try to break quorum by getting 11 senators out of town. There was great excitement. Westbrook calling "Woods—Woods" on sleepers[,] awakening everyone—long distance 'phone calls—our men awakened etc.

It is more likely that attempts to break the quorum were not on June 28, as this entry implies, but on the evening of Friday the 27th, since this was when the critical vote took place. The press reported that during the Friday session the opposition was desperate enough to try to convince eleven senators to resign on June 27 and eliminate the quorum.[134]

In notes Jane McCallum made years later of the exciting times she had shared with Nell Doom, she recalled the scene.

[W]hen [the] Senate saw [that the] only way to delay (near or on week end) and try to win opponents was to break quorum, *they did that* very

---

[133]Senator J. M. Alderdice was from Waxahachie in Ellis County, and Senator James H. Woods resided in Corsicana, Navarro County. They were joined in this vote by Senator W. D. Suiter of Wood County (*Austin Statesman,* June 28, 1919, p. 1; *Members of the Texas Legislature,* 263, 266).

[134]*Austin Statesman,* June 28, 1919, p. 1.

thing. [I remember] Our trip to [the] train on tracks with sargeant at arms who pulled 2 out from under [their] seats & marched [']em up up again— to the capitol. *It passed.* We didn't want to humiliate them so kept at a respectful (giggling I suspect—we were pretty young) distance.[135]

[July 2, 1919]

R.[ail] R.[oad] Commissioner Earl[e] Mayfield's phone call to me and message to Mrs. Cunningham about $5000[00] a year position.

Engagement for him to come to office tomorrow

[July 3 and 4, 1919]

Mr. Mayfield almost begged Minnie to take position which requirements we asked to see ~~state~~ are that place must be filled by a *"pipe line expert."* Had some quiet fun over it.

Altho she needs so much to have a position [I] was so happy to see that this offer with strings to it had no appeal[136] Of course Mayfield wants to run for governor and of course this was his astute(?) method of influencing leader of women to obtain their vote

Thomason is our man, and is very likely to make the race.[137] He is honest, clean and has right ideals. Not overly brilliant but such an improvement over anything we've had in ages.

[July 31, Aug. 1 and 2, 1919]

Have decided fully and finally that despite the efforts, offers and imploring of friends I cannot stand for election to the Presidency of Women Voters League in Texas at October convention. We have the vote and I *must* give my time to my household. As I wrote Minnie (Mrs. Cunningham) in my humble estimation the Lord never gave a woman finer material to work with than he has me; my children need me and want me; and God willing they are going to have me.

"Daddy," bless his bones, would be willing for me to undertake the leadership, for he sees that it can be made the greatest political power in

[135]JYM, "Nell & Others," McCP, II.

[136]Minnie Fisher Cunningham had few or no financial resources upon which to draw. This problem created difficulties from time to time for her and for the state suffrage organization. See Neiuwenhuizen, "Minnie Fisher Cunningham and Jane Y. McCallum," 77-80.

[137]Thomason lost in the 1920 gubernatorial primary. Mayfield did not make the race (Gould, *Progressives and Prohibitionists*, 271). Thomason had a successful career in government, however, as mayor of El Paso, congressman for sixteen years, and federal judge (Texas Legislative Council, *Presiding Officers of the Texas Legislature: 1846-1982* [Austin, 1982], 157).

the state and he likes to have me do things, but he too, is somewhat relieved by my decision to turn my back on the temptation.

When ratification of the Susan B. Anthony amendment put the Texas Equal Suffrage Association out of business, many of those who had been active in that group recognized that they could continue to serve Texans as lobbyists and expand their role in voter education. These battle-tested citizens held a convention in the fall to celebrate victory and to organize the Texas League of Woman Voters. During the intervening summer months several potential leaders had emerged to head up the new group.

Minnie Fisher Cunningham was among those urging Jane McCallum to accept the presidency. Jessie Daniel Ames was not. She wrote that there were two possible candidates for the job: one unnamed woman who "loves honor and destinction and newspaper notoriet[y]" and another (perhaps McCallum) who was "good but weak and very ineffective and incompetent." She wanted to see Minnie Fisher Cunningham in the post, provided that she could have a salary.[138]

McCallum elaborated on her decision to withdraw from the race in a letter to her longtime friend, Ella Dibrell.

[O]thers were so urgent in their demand that I prepare to be a "candidate" for the place that I find it necessary to let my intentions become known *once and for all*. I could not possibly accept the honor under any circumstances. That it is a great, and responsible honor, I am in a position to thoroughly understand. That it will require a thorough knowledge of the State political situation, an unselfish devotion to the cause regardless of personal friendships and ambitions and an acquaintance with the tried and true suffragists all over the State goes without saying. I could probably qualify in these particulars, but in addition, to make it what it *should* be and *must* be if organized, the greatest power for clean government the State of Texas has ever had, it would require unlimited time and attention. This I cannot give. I have fought unceasingly for four years now, and for at least two more my time is to be given to my family.

[138]Minnie Fisher Cunningham to JYM, [Summer 1919], Flagstaff, Ariz., McCP, II; Jessie Daniel Ames to Mrs. Knox, July 17, 1919, McCP, II. The second woman Ames described is possibly Jane McCallum, since Ames refers to this person as Mrs. Cunningham's choice. It is not clear how vigorously Cunningham was advocating McCallum for the post.

As you know, I'll have three sons in the University next year, and they need and want their mother, and D.[eo] V.[olente] they are *going to have her*.[139]

Thus freed from formal responsibilities, Jane McCallum indulged herself for the remainder of 1919 by enjoying her family to the utmost.

[Aug. 4, 1919]
One day this week Alvaro took Henry and me for delightful trip up Lake.
Landed on rocks in Bull Creek ate supper & returned by moonlight.
Alvaro wants to go to School of mines in Colorado year from now.

[Aug. 13, 1919]
Arthur will surely come from wheat fields (where he has been with Frasier Moss since first of June) shortly now. They have stood by their men's jobs like the *real article*, most boys soon get enough of it but how I *ache* to see the boy!

[Aug. 14, 1919]
"Brownie Boy" is still "trying his wings." Bless his heart, he came near running away he was so impatient to get away and do something. He is having his knocks and [I] hope and pray they are good for him.

[Aug. 16 and 17, 1919]
The cat's out. As I stood in Van Smith's (now Woody Gilberts) drug store with Kathleen[,] Earl[e] Mayfield of the $5000[00] "pipe line expert" offer informed me he'd been anxious to see me for several days etc. To make long story short "I am coming out for governor myself" he announced. "I had no business withdrawing from the race last time. I'm not afraid of Thomason or any of them" "How interesting, the more the merrier," was my response. "Well, I want a talk with you before you women pledge to anybody" he continued. "That will be a long time," said I, "for, you know the first lesson we learned in politics was not to pledge at all." He then admonished me as to the necessity of our standing for right man against Ferguson-Bailey combine etc.

[139]JYM to Ella Dibrell, Aug. 10, 1919, folder of letters to and from JYM on suffrage, 1916-1925, McCP, II.

[The day "Thursday" is crossed out on this next page and replaced by McCallum's "Wednesday." "1919" is changed to "1918." She explains why.]

[Oct. 30, 1919]

When I changed the above it was expecting my then soldier boy to use it, beginning on date specified. He had heard 5 boys say they had seen his name on list recommended for officer's training camp, so was expecting to leave *any* day, and I gave him this book.

[Succeeding dates through November 25 are similarly altered.]

[Nov. 26, 1919]

Mr. M. left for St.[ate] Teachers Ass.[ociation] at Houston. Kathleen got in at 7.40 from Taylor. Al Deviney took her to D.[elta] E.[psilon] K.[appa] dance and she got in again at 2 'oclock A.M.. We slept together and had such a good time talking.

[Nov. 27, 1919]

All anticipation, excitement[,] confusion over A. & M game. Train left at 7.30 so I got up at 6 to get them all off. Annie Lewis Preston & a crowd came by for Kathleen. Albert Penn was to take Alvaro, but so late he & Brown went down with *Frazier Moss* while I rang Penn phone fully 5 minutes—Mary Lee coming out with me while Hubert away. We will go to H.[igh] S.[chool] game

[Nov. 28, 1919]

Gloom—gloom—gloom! A & M won 7 - 0. Children all got in last night—last one at 2.30 oclock. M[ary Lee] & I *sat up*. Would have gone to train but it was so late. I've been my *cheerfulest*, and the youngsters are *some* brighter—show *some* symptoms of recovery, but as Alvaro says they'll never get over it until they beat 'em at their own home in *1921*.[140]

[Nov. 29, 1919]

Charlie [Freeman] came over on Texas special. He is *one* persistent lover if one ever lived. Bless his heart, I think a lot of him, but K.[athleen] doesn't.

Mr. M got in early this A.M. much to my delight.

[140]It was humiliating to University of Texas fans that their team extended Texas A & M's season-long streak of not being scored upon (*Austin American*, Nov. 28, 1919, p. 1). The site of this traditionally intense rivalry alternates between Austin and College Station.

[Sunday, Nov. 30, 1919]

Had turkey and ambrosia and other Thanksgiving eats today and the old four, Hubert, M.L.[,] Charlie & Kathleen together at dinner (besides regular family) again[.] Mr. M. & Hubert both said turkey best they'd ever tasted.

[Bottom of page torn, including some manuscript.]

[Dec. 7, 1919]

National Guardsmen coming in so Brown had to drive truck all day meeting soldiers, taking them to town etc. Drove a load of officers & men by home and let them wait in front while he calmly came in for a sweater! On last trip from town went by for Floyd Crosby & North Millican, then for 2 University girls, Mary Marley and Nell Cochran and took them in that lumbering old truck nearly to Camp. North's auto followed & brought the bunch back. Brown may be counted on to have his fun.

Night   (over)
[Dec. 8, 1919]

Old Brown came in so tired that I went to bed with him and petted and talked him to sleep like he was a baby with *all* his 6,' 1 ¼" height.

Had a *long* confidential talk with Alvaro at noon as we sat on kitchen stoop "sunning" ourselves this delightful day. My big old boy! He is having a new experience.

Artie [Jr.] told me some deplorable things about the ease with which students are obtaining whiskey.

How I thank God for our children, and that we are close together. If they'll just remain the same true, clean fellows our lives will not have been in vain.

JANE Y. McCALLUM: 1878-1957

A CHRONOLOGY

1878
Jane LeGette Yelvington was born on December 30, in LaVernia, Wilson County, Texas, the eldest surviving child of Alvaro Leonard and Mary LeGette Yelvington.

The dates of Jane Yelvington's attendance at public schools in Wilson County and her year at Zealey's Female College in Mississippi are unknown.

1896
Jane Yelvington and Arthur Newell McCallum were married on October 29 in LaVernia's Presbyterian church.

1897
The McCallums' first child and only daughter, Kathleen, was born in LaVernia in July, shortly before the family moved to Kenedy, Texas. Arthur McCallum held the post of school superintendent in Kenedy, while Jane helped to stage plays and supplemented the family income by teaching elocution classes.

1900
Son Alvaro Yelvington was born in February. The family moved to the larger town of Seguin when Arthur was named school superintendent there. During her years in Seguin, Jane McCallum participated in the Shakspere Club and helped establish the Village Improvement Society, which built community club rooms and saw to it that trees were planted along town streets.

1901
In November Arthur Newell, Jr., was born in Seguin, Texas.

1903
Jane McCallum was president of Seguin's Shakspere Club when the family made its last major move during the summer. Arthur, Sr., was chosen superintendent of the Austin Public Schools. Their fourth child,

Brown, named for his paternal grandfather, was born in October. In November Alvaro Leonard Yelvington, Jane McCallum's father, died.

1904
McCallum began attending meetings of Austin's Shakspere Club.

1905
The family's home was at 1702 Congress Avenue, according to the city directory. The Colonial Dames of America in Texas accepted Jane McCallum for membership.

1907
The family resided at 2608 Rio Grande. While pregnant with her fifth and last child, Henry DeRosset, who was born in October, Jane McCallum busied herself choosing the words for a spelling text. In December Catherine Maria LeGette, known as Grandmère, died.

1908
The McCallums moved to their new home at 507 (later renumbered as 613) West 32nd Street. The *New Century Spelling Book*, by A. N. McCallum and Houston School Superintendent P. W. Horn was published by Silver, Burdett & Co.

1909
The Mothers' Club at Wooldridge Elementary School gave Jane Y. McCallum the role of treasurer. She chaired the committee on prizes for the Colonial Dames in Texas.

1912
Jane McCallum visited her husband's relatives in North Carolina during the summer, accompanied by four-year-old Henry. Austin's Shakspere Club elected her president. She enrolled at the University of Texas in the fall semester, at age thirty-three.

1913
Kathleen registered at Sweet Briar College in Virginia for the year, while her mother stayed on at the University of Texas. When she accepted membership in Alpha Delta Pi, Jane McCallum became the first married woman to join a University of Texas sorority.

1914
On October 20 McCallum joined the Austin Woman Suffrage Association. She also served on the social committee of the Shakspere Club and attended university classes and meetings of the Colonial Dames.

1915
As winner of the Fine Arts League Prize, Jane McCallum's essay on Elisabet Ney was published in *The Texas Magazine*, a university student periodical. She was elected president of the Austin Woman Suffrage Association in October.

1916
McCallum's earliest surviving diary begins on October 13. She kept up her varied club memberships, was again elected to lead the local suffrage group, and began making speeches on suffrage.

1917
A full diary exists for this year. In January McCallum headlined the program of a successful suffrage luncheon for legislators. This was a prelude to her lobbying activities during the regular session of the state legislature.

Anti-vice work (eliminating the prostitutes from the areas around army training camps) began in June. The separate men's and women's anti-vice groups in Austin merged, with McCallum acting as first vice president. McCallum's other labors in the war effort included helping the Red Cross, raising funds for its work on Tag Day in October, teaching canning methods, and selling liberty bonds in the first and second Liberty Loan campaigns.

As relations between Governor James Ferguson and the University of Texas deteriorated, Jane McCallum began to speak more openly against Ferguson. In June she attended a pro-University meeting in Dallas, and in July she organized and presided over the "Women of Texas Protest" rally at the capitol.

The publication of a letter to the editor of the *Austin American* near the end of June was the first of her contributions to that newspaper. Her weekly column, entitled "Suffrage Corner," ran from July 1 to year's end. In October she was appointed to the board of the Texas Equal Suffrage Association (TESA) as a committee chairperson.

1918

The campaign for prohibition in Austin, in which Jane McCallum lent a hand as secretary of the Woman's Committee, ended happily for her in January.

During the months of February and March McCallum spared no effort lobbying for the primary suffrage bill. Governor Hobby's signature signalled the start of voter registration and education drives. Among the groups devoted to these purposes was the Good Government League, in which she served as vice chairperson. On June 26 Jane McCallum registered to vote. After she cast her ballot in July, she was elected a delegate from Austin's fourth ward to the Travis County Democratic Convention.

In April McCallum helped to form local Hobby clubs, and campaigned for the reelection of Governor William P. Hobby. She also supported Annie Webb Blanton, the first woman to run for statewide office, in the race for state superintendent of public instruction.

Jane Y. McCallum continued writing for the *American* through the first two months of the year. In mid-March her first "Woman and Her Ways" column appeared in the *Austin Statesman*. This work kept her name in the paper weekly throughout the rest of the year.

In early May McCallum agreed to arrange the program for the TESA convention in Austin later in the month. At that meeting members elected her to the executive board as second auditor. In anticipation of the campaign for ratification of the federal (Susan B. Anthony) suffrage amendment, the TESA board later in the year named her to chair its ratification committee.

War work continued unabated during 1918. McCallum performed Red Cross duties and was district women's chairman of the Fourth Liberty Loan drive in October. The Woman's Committee of the Travis County Council of National Defense designated her as chairman of its education committee.

Diary entries for the year conclude with July 20.

1919

In brief diary entries, McCallum managed to record only a portion of her activities for the year. She worked nearly full time through June for the suffrage cause: first, as chairperson of TESA's press and publicity committee for the May 24 referendum on the full suffrage amendment to the state constitution, and later in lobbying the state legislature to ratify the Susan B. Anthony amendment to the U.S. Constitution. "Woman and Her Ways" appeared weekly in the *Austin Statesman* until mid-May.

1920
McCallum gave speeches for Pat Neff during his winning gubernatorial primary campaign against erstwhile suffrage opponent and former U.S. Senator Joseph Weldon Bailey. She was secretary for the Travis County Democratic convention and headed up publicity efforts for the state League of Woman Voters convention in Ft. Worth. By this time she had joined the Kwill Klub. As secretary of the Better Schools Campaign, she successfully promoted a state constitutional amendment which permitted tax increases to benefit rural schools.

1921
Under the title, "Our Austin Correspondent," McCallum began contributing to The New Citizen, a publication of the Texas League of Women Voters. She was district vice-chairman of the Woodrow Wilson Memorial Fund, responsible for raising an endowment for the Woodrow Wilson Foundation. McCallum worked on a history of the suffrage movement in Texas. She did not add significantly to her diary, as two entries were her year's output.

1922
In addition to continuing her column for The New Citizen, McCallum was a member of the Travis County Council of Women. A few diary entries document her activities for this year.

1923
McCallum assumed the duties of executive secretary of the Women's Joint Legislative Council, a cooperative effort of several state women's organizations to influence legislation of interest to them. In the Thirty-eighth Legislature the Petticoat Lobby, as the council was nicknamed, was successful in getting bills enacted which authorized surveys of the state's educational and penal systems, strengthened prohibition laws, and appropriated funds for public schools.

McCallum represented the state League of Women Voters on the Texas Council of Statewide Social Agencies. She handled publicity for the League's convention in San Antonio and continued writing for The New Citizen. In August the Travis County Council of Women named her chairman of its Department of Citizenship.

1924
In February McCallum represented the Kwill Klub at the state Centennial Convention, a planning group which was to organize the celebration

of the Texas Centennial in 1936. She contributed "Woman and Her Ways" columns to the *Austin Statesman* during February.

In March, the same month that she enrolled in University of Texas courses, she was asked to join a committee planning a new football stadium for the campus, to be known as Memorial Stadium.

By this year, McCallum was more active in local Democratic party politics. She was a member of the credentials committee of the Travis County Convention Committee and supported the city manager plan of government for Austin.

In the Texas League of Woman Voters she performed the duties of first vice president and chairman of publicity. McCallum also served as a member of the Texas Committee on Prisons and Prison Labor, which began its work in 1924 and finished in 1927.

1925
In this year of the Thirty-ninth Legislature Jane Y. McCallum again had her work cut out as executive secretary of the Joint Legislative Council. Its program was again enacted, including bills appropriating funds for maternity and infant care, reorganizing the prison system, and strengthening existing child labor laws.

Scant diary material exists for this year.

1926
The few diary entries for this year reflect the fact that McCallum had started researching and writing her book, *Women Pioneers*. Beginning in March she presided over a campaign organization known as the Texas Women Citizens' Committee, Dan Moody for Governor. By the end of the month illness had forced her to resign as executive secretary of the Joint Legislative Council. McCallum's first grandchild, Jane Darling Morley, was born in April to Kathleen and her husband John. Seven more grandchildren would eventually join the extended family.

1927
Governor Dan Moody was inaugurated in January and named Jane Y. McCallum his secretary of state, the second woman to be named to the position. Not long after McCallum took up her post, she discovered an original copy of the Texas Declaration of Independence in an office vault. In addition to learning about preserving and exhibiting this historic document, she set about modernizing procedures and equipment in the Secretary of State's Office. Sparse diary materials exist for this year.

1928
The national Democratic convention was held in Houston in 1928. McCallum served on the Honorary State Reception Committee and was an alternate delegate. The Secretary of State also lent her name to Minnie Fisher Cunningham's bid for the U.S. Senate.

By this date McCallum had joined the Austin Woman's Club and the American Association of University Women.

1929
Dan Moody was reelected governor and reappointed McCallum as secretary of state. Her book, *Women Pioneers*, which portrayed women who had made significant contributions to the settlement of the United States, was brought out by Johnson Publishing Company.

1930
During this tenth anniversary year of the proclamation of the Susan B. Anthony Amendment, McCallum officiated as chairperson for Texas of the League of Woman Voters Memorial Project. She also chaired the program of a reunion suffrage luncheon in March. The public unveiling of the Texas Declaration of Independence in its specially constructed shrine in the capitol took place on March 2.

1931
When Governor Ross Sterling reappointed McCallum in January, she became the first person to serve as secretary of state under two governors. Delta Kappa Gamma, an honorary woman educators' society founded by Annie Webb Blanton and others in 1929, elected her to membership. McCallum's "Woman and Her Ways" appeared weekly between February and May in the *Austin American-Statesman*.

1932
The Texas Fine Arts Association asked McCallum to join its library committee and help upgrade the Elisabet Ney Museum. She assisted in Ross Sterling's reelection campaign by giving radio speeches. His opponent, Miriam A. ("Ma") Ferguson, defeated him in the primary.

1933
McCallum's diary for this year leads off with her leaving office at the state capitol. In November she was chosen historian of the local chapter of the Colonial Dames in Texas. Illness late in the year forced her to resign

her membership on the local National Recovery Administration compliance board. In the last days of the year she had gall bladder surgery.

1934
McCallum began 1934 with a stay at the Mayo Clinic in Rochester, Minnesota. Later in the year the recurrence of her illness necessitated her resignation from the Travis County Consumers Council, and she returned to the Mayo Clinic in August. Jane McCallum's "Mamma," Mary LeGette Yelvington, died in December. A very limited number of diary entries exist for this year.

1935
After being elected its historian, McCallum was elevated to the state executive board of the National Society of Colonial Dames. She was also a member of the board of the Travis County Council of Women.

1936
McCallum was appointed a director of the Texas Public Safety Council. She helped to plan a county tuberculosis hospital as a member of the central committee for the project.

1939
As second vice president of the Austin Federated Women's Clubs, McCallum worked to raise funds for the Austin-Travis County Tuberculosis Sanatorium, which opened in May 1940. Mrs. Willie D. Bowles, a University of Texas graduate student, conducted research in the McCallum home for her Master's thesis on woman suffrage, using TESA records which were stored in the attic.

1940
Interspersed among the tallies for countless domino games in this year's so-called diary are notes made by Jane McCallum and others. She was named a presidential elector, casting her vote for Roosevelt and Wallace at the same session in which she supported a resolution to abolish the electoral college.

1941
Congressman Lyndon Johnson, with McCallum's endorsement, was a candidate for the U.S. Senate in the primary race against Governor W. Lee O'Daniel.

1942
Arthur Newell McCallum, Sr., retired in June, ending a thirty-nine-year career as superintendent of Austin Public Schools. In July Jane McCallum functioned as acting state chairman of the Dan's the Man for Senate committee, demonstrating her continued backing of former Governor Moody.

1943
Beginning in March and continuing for several years, McCallum contributed a weekly "Women and War" column to the *Austin American-Statesman*. A. N. McCallum, Sr., died on November 20. Jane McCallum's diary records her constant attention at his bedside and visits from family members as his health declined.

1944
In May McCallum was named a Democratic state committeewoman, representing the Tenth U.S. Congressional District on the executive committee. She assisted in her friend Minnie Fisher Cunningham's run for the governor's mansion, beginning in June.

1945
The Women's Committee for Educational Freedom was organized in January under McCallum's chairmanship. Its stated objectives were: 1) the reinstatement of Homer P. Rainey as president of the University of Texas; 2) the resignation of the regents who had approved his dismissal in November 1944; and 3) the revision of the laws under which regents were selected.

This year was McCallum's first to hold a seat on the Austin Planning Commission.

1946
McCallum resigned from the state Democratic executive committee.

1948
In January McCallum worked as co-chair of Women's Day during Rededication Week, a patriotic reminder of American ideals. She visited the Freedom Train with the mayor's party when it stopped in Austin in February. In addition to doing research for a manuscript which she called "All Texians Were Not Males," McCallum actively supported Lyndon

Johnson in his U.S. Senate race. She kept a diary faithfully for the first two months of the year.

1949
The Colonial Dames in Texas gave McCallum the job of chairing its nominating committee this year.

1950
In a fairly complete diary for the year, McCallum wrote of her continuing work on her manuscript and her service on Austin's Planning Commission.

1952
A fire in the attic of the family home in December 1951 gave Jane McCallum the incentive to reread and sort through many of her papers which had been stored there. She kept up with her diary as she negotiated unsuccessfully for the publication of "All Texians Were Not Males." While construction proceeded on a public high school to be named in honor of her husband, she collected materials about him.

Her labors in behalf of the more liberal underdogs in politics placed her on the losing side in both the Ralph Yarborough vs. Alan Shivers gubernatorial primary and the Adlai Stevenson vs. Dwight Eisenhower presidential election. McCallum chaired her precinct for the local Democratic party.

This was McCallum's last year of service on the Planning Commission. She was thrilled to see her children, their spouses, and her grandchildren as they visited for holidays or stopped by unexpectedly while traveling through town.

1953
The dedication of McCallum High School took place in September.

1954
Jane McCallum was named Commissioner of the Travis County Grand Jury in November, the first woman to hold this post.

1957
Jane Yelvington McCallum died on August 15 at age seventy-eight. In tribute to her life and career, flags at the city hall and state capitol were lowered to half staff.

PUBLISHED WORKS BY
JANE Y. MCCALLUM

This chronologically arranged list is by no means exhaustive. Much of Jane Y. McCallum's published writing appeared in newpapers and is difficult to retrieve. As press and publicity chairman for two suffrage campaigns, her press releases were distributed statewide. They were edited locally and often were reproduced without a byline.

"Builder of Formosa." *The Texas Magazine* 31 (Oct. 1915):17-19.

Letter to the Editor. *Austin American*, June 30[?], 1917.

"The Suffrage Corner." *Austin American*. This column appeared weekly from July 1, 1917, to Jan. 27, 1918.

"Austin Women Show Pleasure at Victory of Suffrage Cause." *Austin American*, Jan. 11, 1918, p. 2. McCallum contributed to this article. See the diary entry for Jan. 21, 1918.

"Austin Suffragists Watching for the Senate to Vote." *Austin American*, Feb. 3, 1918, p. 17.

"Austin Suffragists after Culberson to 'Vote for Women.'" *Austin American*, Feb. 10, 1918, p. 11.

"Texas Suffrage a Right of War and Aid to U.S." *Austin American*, Mar. 3, 1918, p. 10.

"Mothers of Austin Tell Why They Favor Votes For Women." *Austin American*, Mar. 10, 1918.

"Woman and Her Ways." *Austin Statesman*. This column appeared weekly from Mar. 17, 1918, to May 18, 1919.

"Notes on Suffrage Meeting." *Austin Statesman*, May 28, 1918, p. 4.

"Women in Politics." *Austin Statesman*. This column appeared on July 2, 3, and 5, 1918.

"The Woman Voter." *Austin Statesman*. This column appeared on July 24, 25, and 26, 1918.

"Special to The News." *Dallas Morning News*, Mar. 16, 1919, p. 3. The press release from which this unsigned article was written was also the basis for a nearly identical article in the *San Antonio Express*, Mar. 16, 1919, p. 5. See the diary entry for Mar. 15, 1919.

"Speaker Strongly Endorses Woman Suffrage for Texas Women." *Austin Statesman*, Mar. 20, 1919, p. 6.

"Our Austin Correspondent." *The New Citizen*. This column appeared in the newsletter of the Texas League of Women Voters between April 1921 and July 1924.

"Formosa: The Unique Haven of a Strange and Gifted Exile." *Holland's Magazine*, Jan. 1922, 16, 34.

"Texas." *In The History of Woman Suffrage*, edited by Elizabeth Cady Stanton, Susan B. Anthony, Matilda Joslyn Gage, and Ida Husted Harper, vol. 6, 630-43. New York: National American Woman Suffrage Association, 1881-1922.

"Woman and Her Ways." *Austin Statesman*. This weekly column began on February 3, 1924, and expanded to a full page format on March 3. The last contribution in this series was on April 27, 1924.

"Women in Politics." *London Times, Texas Supplement*, Mar. 31, 1925, p. ix. This special supplement was printed "in honor of the International Convention of the Associated Advertising Clubs," which was meeting in Houston at the time.

Handbook for Organizers. N.p., n.d. This pamphlet was used in Dan Moody's 1926 gubernatorial campaign. McCallum indicated that she was the author on the copy which is in the McCallum Papers, Part II, Austin History Center, Austin Public Library.

Women Pioneers. New York: Johnson Publishing Company, 1929.

"Why Put a Lot of Doubt on Independence Declaration?" *Austin Statesman*, Mar. 2, 1929, pp. 1, 11.

"The Texas Field for Writers." *Alcalde*, May 1930, 327-28.

Biennial Report of the Secretary of State of the State of Texas: September 1, 1929, to September 1, 1930. Austin, n.d.

"Woman and Her Ways." *Austin American-Statesman*. This weekly series began on February 22, 1931, and continued until April 26, 1931.

"Home Eco Building To Be Texas Museum and Laboratory, Too." *Austin American-Statesman*, Apr. 24, 1932, Society sect., pp. 1, 3.

"Activities of Women in Texas Politics." In *Texas Democracy: A Centennial History of Politics and Personalities of the Democratic Party, 1836-1936*, edited by Frank Carter Adams, 466-93. Austin: Democratic Historical Association, 1937. Reprinted in A. Elizabeth Taylor, Ruthe Winegarten, and Judith N. McArthur, *Citizens at Last: The Woman Suffrage Movement in Texas*. Austin: Ellen C.Temple, 1987, 202-30.

"The Fight of U.S. Women for Right to Vote Is Story Packed With Pathos, Humor, Determination." *Houston Post*, Aug. 25, 1940.

Letter to the Editor. *Austin American-Statesman*, Feb. 28, 1943, Society sect., p. 6.

Letter to the Editor. *Austin American-Statesman*, Mar. 14, 1943, Society sect., p. 6.

"Women and War." *Austin American-Statesman*. This column appeared weekly with very few exceptions (save for the period when Arthur N. McCallum, Sr., died) from March 21, 1943, to September 23, 1945. It deals with issues of interest to women, including current politics and history as well as women's role in wartime and their hopes for peace.

"Eve in the New Era." *Austin American-Statesman*. This column picked up from where "Women and War" left off, appearing each Sunday from September 30, 1945, to March 16, 1947. Topics ranged farther: mental health, education, Frances Perkins, the Petticoat Lobby, moonlight towers, Eleanor Roosevelt, growth issues in Austin, and prohibition.

"The Alamo Had One." *Houston Post* [Dec. 1948?]. A copy of this article and the press release (dated December 12, 1948) on which it is based are located in Box 6, McCallum Papers, II, Austin History Center.

"Colonial Dames of America (Texas Branch)"; "Charles B. Metcalfe"; "Woman Suffrage"; "Women's Joint Legislative Council." In *Handbook of Texas*, edited by Walter Prescott Webb and H. Bailey Carroll. 2 vols. Austin: The Texas State Historical Association, 1952.

"Elisabet Ney's Bequest Derives Growing Interest." *Texas Fine Arts News* 2 (Dec. 19, 1945):1-2.

"The School Marm Said It First." *Texas Parade* 14 (Nov. 1953):1-2.

"All Texans Were Not Males." *Texas Parade* 16 (Sept. 1955):19-20.

SELECTED BIBLIOGRAPHY

Manuscript Sources

Austin File (AF)-Biography. Vertical files. Austin History Center, Austin Public Library.

Austin Woman Suffrage Association. Minute book, 1908-1914. Barker Texas History Center, University of Texas at Austin.

Cunningham, Minnie Fisher. Papers. Houston Metropolitan Research Center, Houston Public Library.

> This collection of twenty-five boxes includes records of the Texas Equal Suffrage Association (1915-1920), correspondence from most Texas counties (1915-1920), and correspondence from Jane Y. McCallum to Minnie Fisher Cunningham.

McCallum, Arthur N., Sr., and Jane Y. McCallum. Papers. Private collection of Betty Jane McCallum Ozbun, Austin, Texas.

> The collection contains note cards for speeches given by Arthur N. McCallum while superintendent of the Austin Public Schools and Jane Y. McCallum's diaries and record books for 1919, 1927, January 1939 and January 1940 (with an entry for D-Day), and 1943 (misdated as 1942).

McCallum, Jane Y. Papers, Part I. Austin History Center, Austin Public Library. Formerly titled McCallum Family Papers.

> This collection of nine linear feet (roughly 15,000 pages) includes McCallum's diaries for October 13, 1916-July 20, 1918, December 1920-December 1926, 1933-34, 1948, 1950, and 1952; family correspondence; materials from McCallum's press and publicity committee for the 1919 referendum on woman suffrage, the League of Woman Voters Tenth Anniversary Memorial Project (1930), Dan Moody's 1926 gubernatorial campaign, and the Women's Committee for Educational Freedom (1945); some of Minnie Fisher Cunningham's post-1920 letters to McCallum; and clippings and photographs from Cunningham's election campaign.

> There are a great many state suffrage papers including a scrapbook of Texas Equal Rights Association clippings (1893-94); the TERA treasurer's book (1903-16); correspondence of Annette Finnigan (1914-15) and Minnie Fisher Cunningham (1915-19); newspaper clip-

pings on suffrage from around the state; handbills and bulletins from the National American Woman Suffrage Association; photographs of a number of state and national suffrage leaders; drafts and finished versions of several suffrage histories written by McCallum, Willie D. Bowles, and A. Elizabeth Taylor; and A. Caswell Ellis's papers on suffrage (articles, speeches, letters, clippings).

McCallum, Jane Y. Papers, Part II. Austin History Center, Austin Public Library.

This collection of twenty-eight linear feet (roughly 50,000 pages) contains three broad categories of documents:

1. Personal McCallum papers, including family correspondence; family history and genealogical information; lecture notes and compositions from university courses; materials from organizations of which McCallum was a member; letters from Minnie Fisher Cunningham; research notes and drafts of articles; Arthur N. McCallum, Sr.'s family correspondence, clippings, and tributes.

2. Papers relating to McCallum's public offices and campaigns, including materials on Liberty Loan drives; the Good Government Campaign (1917); Better Schools Campaign (1920); Woodrow Wilson Foundation; Texas League of Woman Voters (1920s); Joint Legislative Council (background reports on issues, correspondence, press releases, and financial records for 1923-26); Texas Committee on Prisons and Prison Labor (1924-27); NRA Compliance Board (1933); and Women's Committee for Educational Freedom (1945).

There are political campaign materials (correspondence, publicity, propaganda, speeches, clippings) for the gubernatorial elections of 1926 through 1934, and Dan Moody's 1942 U.S. Senate race; and materials from McCallum's service on the state Democratic executive committee, city charter revision commission, and city planning commission.

The secretary of state's papers consist of correspondence, clippings, and reports for 1928 through January 1933.

3. Papers of the Texas Equal Suffrage Association, including correspondence of Annette Finnigan to local chapters, individuals, and the National American Woman Suffrage Association (1914-15), Perle Penfield (1914-15), Minnie Fisher Cunningham (1915-19), Lavinia Engle (1916-17), Lutie Sterns (1916-17), and Helen Moore (1916-18); financial records and treasurer's correspondence (1915-19) from Anna Walker and Jessie Daniel Ames; press releases and correspon-

dence on publicity for the 1919 referendum written by McCallum; association records (minutes of meetings, printed brochures, petitions on woman suffrage submitted to the Thirty-fourth Legislature; and lists of legislators, newspapers, and contact people).

McCallum, Jane Y. Papers. Barker Texas History Center, University of Texas at Austin.

These documents (two inches, or roughly 300 pages), which concern the Texas Declaration of Independence, include newspaper clippings, correspondence about the preservation and display of the document, and information on the signers.

Pennybacker, Mrs. Percy V. (Anna J.). Papers. Barker Texas History Center, University of Texas at Austin.

PUBLISHED PRIMARY SOURCES

Austin City Directory. Title, city of publication, and publisher vary. 1905-1922.

Austin Woman's Christian Temperance Union. *Directory and Cook Book.* N.p., n.d.

Benedict, H.Y., comp. *A Source Book Relating to the History of the University of Texas: Legislative, Legal, Bibliographical, and Statistical,* University of Texas Bulletin, No. 1757: Oct. 10, 1917.

The Cactus. Austin: University of Texas. 1916-1919.

General Register of the Students and Former Students of the University of Texas. Ex-Student's Association: [Austin], 1917.

Papachristou, Judith. *Women Together: A History in Documents of the Women's Movement in the United States.* New York: Alfred A. Knopf, 1976.

NEWSPAPERS

Austin American. 1916-1919.

Austin Statesman. 1916-1919.

London Times, Texas Supplement. Mar. 30, 1925.

Secondary Sources

Boone, Dorothy. "Arthur Newell McCallum." Typescript, Austin History Center, Austin Public Library.

Bowles, Willie D. "History of the Woman Suffrage Movement in Texas." Master's thesis, University of Texas at Austin, 1939. (Copy at Barker Texas History Center, University of Texas at Austin.)

Brown, Norman D. *Hood, Bonnet, and Little Brown Jug*. College Station: Texas A & M University Press, 1984.

Dugger, Ronnie. *Our Invaded Universities: Form, Reform, and New Starts*. New York: W. W. Norton & Co., 1974.

Flexner, Eleanor. *Century of Struggle*. Rev. ed. Cambridge: The Belknap Press of Harvard University Press, 1975.

Fowler, Robert Booth. *Carrie Catt: Feminist Politician*. Boston: Northeastern University Press, 1986.

Franz, Joe B. *The Forty-Acre Follies*. Austin: Texas Monthly Press, 1983.

Gould, Lewis L. *Progressives and Prohibitionists: Texas Democrats in the Wilson Era*. Austin: University of Texas Press, 1973.

___. "The University Becomes Politicized: The War with Jim Ferguson." *Southwestern Historical Quarterly* 86 (1982): 255-76.

Graham, Sally Hunter. "Woodrow Wilson, Alice Paul, and the Woman Suffrage Movement." *Political Science Quarterly* 98 (1983-84): 665-79.

Hall, Jacquelyn Dowd. *Revolt against Chivalry: Jessie Daniel Ames and the Women's Campaign Against Lynching*. New York: Columbia University Press, 1979.

Humphrey, David C. *Austin: An Illustrated History*. Northridge, Ca.: Windsor Publications, 1985.

Jackson, Emma Louise Moyer. "Petticoat Politics: Political Activism among Texas Women in the 1920's." Ph.D. diss., University of Texas at Austin, 1980. (Copy at Austin History Center, Austin Public Library.)

Kennedy, David M. *Over Here: The First World War and American Society*. New York: Oxford University Press, 1980.

Kraditor, Aileen S. *The Ideas of the Woman Suffrage Movement, 1900-1920*. New York: Columbia University Press, 1965.

Leuchtenburg, William E. *The Perils of Prosperity: 1914-32*. Chicago: University of Chicago Press, 1958.

Lunardini, Christine A. *From Equal Suffrage to Equal Rights: Alice Paul and the National Woman's Party, 1910-1928*. New York: New York University Press, 1986.

Members of the Texas Legislature: 1846-1980. N.p., N.d.

Moreland, Sinclair. *Texas Women's Hall of Fame*. Austin: Biographical Press, 1917.

Nieuwenhuizen, Patricia B. "Minnie Fisher Cunningham and Jane Y. McCallum, Leaders of Texas Women for Suffrage and Beyond." Senior thesis, University of Texas at Austin, 1982. (Copies at Barker Texas History Center, University of Texas at Austin and Austin History Center, Austin Public Library.)

Polan, Glenn K. "Minnie Fisher Cunningham." Master's thesis, Sam Houston State University, 1968.

Richmond, Rebecca. *A Woman of Texas: Mrs. Percy V. Pennybacker*. San Antonio: Naylor Co., 1941.

Scott, Anne Firor and Andrew MacKay Scott. *One Half the People: The Fight for Woman Suffrage*. Urbana: University of Illinois Press, 1975.

Sims, Anastasia. "The Woman Suffrage Movement in Texas." Senior thesis, University of Texas at Austin, 1974. (Copy at Barker Texas History Center, University of Texas at Austin.)

Taylor, A. Elizabeth. "The Woman Suffrage Movement in Texas." *Journal of Southern History* 17 (1951): 195-215. Reprinted in A. Elizabeth Taylor, Ruthe Winegarten, and Judith N. McArthur, *Citizens at Last: The Woman Suffrage Movement in Texas*. Austin: Ellen C. Temple, 1987.

Webb, Walter Prescott, H. Bailey Carroll, and Eldon Stephen Branda, eds. *The Handbook of Texas*. 3 vols. Austin: Texas State Historical Association, 1952, 1976.

INDEX

CPSIA information can be obtained at www.ICGtesting.com
Printed in the USA
LVOW06s0108230915

455283LV00001B/3/P